Chris

Grace

A Leader's Guide to a Better Us

Thank you for
inspiring me
to write this book.
Your story has
made it better.

[signature] 5/19

Grace

A Leader's Guide to a Better Us

John Baldoni

Indigo River Publishing

oΟo

ENDORSEMENTS

"Leadership is about humility, love and service. *GRACE: A Leader's Guide to a Better Us* reveals how leaders demonstrate what it means to be open to others, how they care for their people, and how they serve for the 'greater good.' GRACE can be your handbook for creating a stronger culture and a more supportive workplace that enriches your team and your organization's performance."

— Alan Mulally, former CEO of Boeing Commercial Aircraft and Ford Motor Company

"In a moment when it seems that grace is a lost art, a collection of thoughtful leaders and writers have come together to restore it. This book couldn't come at a better time."

— Adam Grant, *New York Times* bestselling author of *Give and Take* and *Originals*.

"One of my favorite sayings is 'Life is good.' In *GRACE: A Leader's Guide to a Better Us,* John Baldoni gives that reality new meaning. *GRACE* contains story after story of women and men taking it upon themselves to make a positive difference in the lives of other people. Grace is a gift that we all need more of it."

— Marshall Goldsmith, world's No. 1 executive coach and author of multiple *New York Times* best-sellers including *What Got You Here, Won't Get You There, Mojo* and *Triggers*

"John Baldoni's excellent book reminds us that leadership is more about attitude than just aptitude. Too often boards focus exclusively on technical skills and not enough on character. Treating people with grace will make everyone a better leader."

— Carlos Gutierrez, co-chair of the Albright Stonebridge Group and former CEO of The Kellogg Company

"*GRACE: A Leader's Guide to a Better Us* is the product of a fruitful career spent immersed in the study and practice of leadership, and it shows. Based on the fundamental notion that the pursuit of profits alone will not give us everything we need, John Baldoni gets to the heart of what's too often missing: grace, the catalyst for pursuing the greater good. Through stories big and small, Baldoni reveals what it takes to live and lead with grace in ways that can have a profound impact on those around you – and yourself. If you feel like there must be something more, this book will help you find it."

— John U. Bacon, author of the National Bestseller, *The Great Halifax Explosion*

"John Baldoni brings grace to life in his outstanding new book! Laced with a myriad of inspiring stories and examples, there is no doubt that grace is real and that it is alive today. *Grace* is the kind of book we desperately need during these times when so many people have forgotten what good leadership looks like. Baldoni shows how to make grace available to each of us so you can become the leader you were meant to be and the kind of leader the world needs today."

— Jesse Lyn Stoner, CEO Seapoint Center, co-author *Full Steam Ahead: Unleash the Power of Vision*

"There is no better time than now to pause and reflect on the power of grace. And there is no better guide for this journey than John Baldoni. Sharing roots from world religions and bringing to life with stories from modern times, Baldoni moves us to feel grace and gives us actionable steps to do more to help others."

— Kevin Kruse, *New York Times* Bestselling Author

"*A Leaders Guide to Better Us* is a consummate book that teaches leaders and upcoming leaders the importance and value of being selfless and compassionate. Leadership has become synonymous with vainglory, but John captures the essence of leadership with a moral striving by capturing the most quintessential elements of leadership: grace, generosity, respect, action, compassion, and energy. This is the perfect book for those seeking to hone their leadership abilities and gain a better understanding of what it takes be a good leader."

— Shermichael Singleton, *Forbes 30 under 30* and *MSNBC* contributor

Indigo River Publishing
3 West Garden Street, Ste. 352
Pensacola, FL 32502
www.indigoriverpublishing.com

Ordering Information:
Quantity sales: Special discounts are available on quantity purchases by corporations, associations, and others. For details, contact the publisher at the address above.

Editors: Deborah DeNicola and Tanner Chau
Cover and interior design: mycustombookcover.com

Orders by US trade bookstores and wholesalers: Please contact the publisher at the address above.

Printed in the United States of America

Library of Congress Control Number: 2019939689

ISBN: 978-1-948080-88-0

First Edition

*With Indigo River Publishing, you can always expect great books, strong voices, and meaningful messages. Most importantly, you'll always find…*words worth reading.

○◯○

ALSO BY JOHN BALDONI

MOXIE: The Secret to Bold and Gutsy Leadership (2015)

The Leader's Guide to Speaking with Presence: How to Project Confidence, Conviction and Authority (2013)

The Leader's Pocket Guide: Indispensable Tools, Tips and Techniques for Any Situation (2012)

Lead With Purpose: Giving Your Organization a Reason to Believe in Itself (2011)

AMA Handbook of Leadership edited by Marshall Goldsmith, John Baldoni and Sarah McArthur (2010)

12 Steps to Power Presence: How to Exert Your Authority to Lead (2010)

Lead Your Boss: The Subtle Art of Managing Up (2009)

Lead By Example: 50 Ways Great Leaders Inspire Results (2008)

How Great Leaders Get Great Results (2006)

Great Motivation Secrets of Great Leaders (2005)

Great Communication Secrets of Great Leaders (2003)

180 Ways to Walk the Motivation Talk (co-author with Eric Harvey) 2002

Personal Leadership: Taking Control of Your Work Life (2001)

180 Ways to Walk the Leadership Talk (2000)

◦○◦

To my son Paul
Who knows what it means to lead with grace

◦○◦

Contents

○◯○

The following women and men—all leaders in their chosen disciplines—provided interviews with the author for this book.

Wayne Baker is a professor of sociology at the Ross School of Business at the University of Michigan. Wayne, together with wife Cheryl, are founders of Give and Take, Inc. The firm creates software that helps companies build a culture of generosity at work, which leads to better employee engagement and productivity.

Louis Carter is CEO and President of Best Practice Institute which provides consulting services to senior executives and organizations. Louis' research focuses on ways organizations can achieve peak performance by adopting positive, values-based behaviors. Louis is the author of more than a dozen books, including his newest the *Emotionally Connected Leader*.

Stephen M. R. Covey is a co-founder of CoveyLink and the FranklinCovey Global Speed of Trust Practice. A sought-after and compelling keynote speaker and adviser on trust, leadership, ethics, sales and high performance, he speaks to audiences around the world. He is the *New York Times* and number one *Wall Street Journal* best-selling author of *The Speed of Trust*, a groundbreaking, paradigm-shifting outlook on trust. Stephen formerly served as the CEO of the Covey Leadership Center.

Sally Helgesen was cited by Forbes as, "the world's premier expert on women's leadership." Sally speaks, coaches, and teaches globally. She is the author of many books including *The Female Advantage: Women's Ways of Leadership*, *The Female Vision: Women's Real Power* *at Work, The Web of Inclusion: A New Architecture for Building Great Organizations* and her newest, co-authored with Marshall Goldsmith, *How Women Rise.*

Dave Johnson Ph.D. is a licensed clinical social worker, marriage and family therapist, and board-certified clinical nurse specialist. He is a Professor of Nursing at the University of Saint Francis and an Employee Assistance Specialist with Parkview Health in Fort Wayne, Indiana. Dave weaves stories and anecdotes that reveal the nature of stress in juggling work and family and strategies for maintaining one's sense of humor and perspective.

Alaina Love is Creator of Passionality® and President and Co-founder of Purpose Linked Consulting. A nationally recognized expert in leadership and individual purpose and passion, Alaina is the co-author of the bestselling McGraw-Hill book, *The Purpose Linked Organization: How Passionate Leaders Inspire Winning Teams and Great Results.*

Chris Lowney, a former Jesuit seminarian and a managing director at Morgan Stanley, serves on the board of CHI, one of the nation's largest hospital systems. Chris is the author of many books on leadership including *Heroic Leadership, Pope Francis: Why He Leads the Way He Leads*, and his newest, *Make Today Matter: 10 Habits for a Better Life.*

Christine Porath is an assistant professor of organizational behavior at the McDonough School of Business at Georgetown University. She consults for many corporate and governmental organizations. Considered a seminal thinker in the role that civility plays in the workplace, Christine is the author of many peer-reviewed management articles, including the *Harvard Business Review* and several books including her newest, *Mastering Civility.*

Mike McKinney is president and CEO of Leadership Now, a

leadership resource provider of books and media for managers and executives. Mike has a strong social media presence which he uses to promote leadership wisdom of many prominent leadership thinkers and writers.

Scott Moorehead is an entrepreneur's entrepreneur. Scott serves as CEO of Round Room, a collection of businesses including TCC, a premium Verizon retailer, as well as a number of technology companies. Scott also heads Culture of Good, a company focused on positive cultural change. He is the co-author of the book *Building Your Culture of Good*, which profiles TCC's efforts to provide every employee with "permission to care" as it relates to creating the "greater good."

Alan Mulally is former CEO of Boeing Commercial Airplanes and Ford Motor Company. As CEO of Ford, Alan led the comeback of the company that restored profitability and saw Ford named as the most respected automotive brand in the world. In 2015 *Fortune* magazine named Alan the No. 3 most respected leader, right behind Pope Francis and Angela Merkel.

Skip Prichard is CEO of OCLC, a leading provider of software for libraries. Skip has also served as CEO of two other firms. A prolific writer and interviewer, Skip is the author of the national best-seller, *Book of Mistakes: 9 Secrets to Creating a Successful Future.*

Tim Sanders is a *New York Times* best-selling author with over one million copies of his five books in print. Considered a key influencer, Tim is a much-in-demand keynote speaker on the themes of leadership, sales and collaboration.

It comes calling
As a light breeze across the tall grasses,
Whispering as it ripples.
Our spirits, like the grasses, are moved.

We call it grace, the disposition to do something more for others. Actions big and small are acts of grace when done with the right intention and the right goals. While grace is perceived to be spiritual, its manifestation is personal. We reveal it in our actions toward others. In other words, grace is like *character*. We can think of it, but it is only evident when we act upon it.

While I have written about grace previously, now seems an especially good time to focus on the topic. Our culture has become more coarsened. The rancor in our political system, fueled as it is by people who do not want to listen to one another, paralyzes so much of our public discourse.

So, if ever there were a time to speak about grace, it is now.

Everyone of us can point to people in our community who resonate grace. These are the men and women who spend their time working to make the lives of others better. Teachers, social workers, and community volunteers who give of themselves without asking why; they see a need and they fulfill it. They do not seek recognition, but it should be our responsibility as citizens to give it to them.

For some, grace is the whisper of a Creator. For others, grace is

XVIII · JOHN BALDONI

the beating of the heart within. It is a call to do more as a means of helping others do what they cannot do. Eat. Wash. Learn. Thrive. People with grace deliver it.

There is another form of grace that we see in the physical world. It is the fluidity of motion that athletes, actors, and dancers possess. It is also the movement that artists give their art—be it a painting or a piece of music. Grace is kinetic, but it is also fluidity and a sense of equilibrium and balance that moves forward.

Grace becomes inspiration, be it in life or in athletics or in art. We look at people with grace and find that their actions motivate us to do something better if only to appreciate what it means to live life by paying attention.

We find grace in joy. Acting in the spirit of grace is deeply joyful. We take joy in making things better for others. Joy also gives us personal happiness. You can say there is grace in the simple enjoyment of a flower, a conversation with a friend, a funny situation. Grace reveals itself in the joy we take in life.

Grace, some say, is love itself. How can you want to do better for others if you do not love them? And you can only love them if you humble yourself. Humility is integral to grace because it teaches us to put others before ourselves. In doing so we acknowledge our limitations but also recognize our capacity to do better.

Grace is spiritual as well as physical. It combines the will to perform with the will to live in ways that renew our sense of community, as participants in life itself.

This book explores grace in five ways; conveniently I have turned the word itself into an acronym.

G is for generosity, *the will to do something for others.*

R is respect, *the dignity of life and work.*

A is action, *the mechanism for change.*

C is compassion, *the concern for others.*

E is energy, *the spirit that catalyzes us.*

Part of the need for grace is our need to stop acting and stop living alone. Our culture reveres autonomy—carve your own way in the world—and that is what has fueled entrepreneurism, the ability to start with nothing and create something of value. Not only do business people do this, so too do artists, writers, designers, and filmmakers. This independence is laudatory and frankly necessary for societies to move forward. We need women and men who will think and act outside of the norm in order to create a better tomorrow.

There are limits, however. Society, as a whole, cannot sustain itself if there is only a collection of self-interested beings. We need to share ourselves with others—colleagues, friends, and family. And while we celebrate the spirit of individualism more perhaps than we do the shared oneness of being human, we are human. We must learn to reach out to one another.

David Brooks in the *New York Times* wrote a column in which he said, "Most of us require communal patterns and shared cultural norms and certain enforced guardrails to help us restrain our desires and keep us free."[1]

Father Greg Boyle, Jesuit priest and founder of the gang intervention program Homeboy Industries, believes in something he calls "radical kinship"— a connectedness that binds one human to another. In the introduction to his book, *Barking to the Choir*, he writes, "Kinship is the game-changer. It is the Pearl of Great Price. It is the treasure buried in the field. Let's sell everything to get it."[2]

Our shared collectivism calls for sublimation of ego at certain times. None of us can, nor should, be on top all of the time. "Me-first-ism" is never healthy; it locks the individual into a form of selfishness that is self-devouring. You can't be satisfied with more things or more followers. Greed is your catalyst and it can wreak a terrible toll—unhappiness and loneliness.

Grace, however, can dissolve our inner sense of reserve. It can be the spirit that enables us to reach out and find a connection with others. Grace comes together in ways that make us better by showing us a better way to behave toward one another as well as how we treat ourselves. Grace is also a journey, and exploration of what comes next, but also a commitment to make that journey—our chosen path—more meaningful.

Grace is a gift . . . for some it comes from a Higher Power. For others, it comes from within. No matter how you view it, grace is uniquely human because it gives us the sense of self to make things better.

Chapter 1

"Will is to grace as the horse is to the rider."

— Saint Augustine

Why Grace?

Grace is the essence of life that enables us to see the world as not simply a place for us but rather a place for all of us. Grace is the awareness that while life is good; it can be made better by us for others. Grace is a gift that we must share readily for without it the world is a darker and more forbidding place.

Long Live the Queen

Quite simply she was the Queen. One who earned 18 Grammys and sold 75 million records. More than that, she oozed her way into the hearts and lives of the Baby Boom generation and their children, too. She was a woman proud of herself and in the process, helped us feel proud, as well. Aretha Franklin, Queen of Soul.

Her father was the famed civil rights preacher C.L. Franklin at Detroit's New Bethel Baptist. Her mother died when Aretha was nine, which was about the time that she was beginning to play piano and sing in her father's church. Aretha grew up surrounded by the songs of gospel, the blues of the South, and the rhythms of jazz. Gospel legends like Clara Ward and Mahalia Jackson were her

2 · JOHN BALDONI

mentors. She also stayed close to what would become the Motown sound. Smokey Robinson and Diana Ross lived nearby.

Aretha was something of a stateswoman of soul. She sang the Gospel hymn "Precious Lord" at the funeral for Martin Luther King, Jr. when she was still in her teens. As an adult, Aretha sang at both of President Bill Clinton's inaugurations and at the first inaugural for Barack Obama when she brought the house down with "My Country 'tis of Thee."

Aretha was a restless performer, not content with staying in one genre. She pushed herself to learn to sing opera. She engaged Mary Callaghan Lynch, a soprano and voice coach, to teach her. And one night at the Grammy awards in 1998, without time to rehearse, she stepped in for an ill Luciano Pavarotti to sing an aria he had made famous, "Nessun Dorma." She began in Italian and finished in English bringing the story of the doomed lovers, in Puccini's *Turandot*, to life in ways that most audiences likely had never heard. An aria with a twist of soul. Their working relationship continued until Aretha's death. While Aretha never did learn to read music, she played by ear and by heart.

It was gospel, however, in which she found True North. Her voice was rich and full, but it could be soft and velvety when she sang of the Lord. She could croon sweetly in "Amazing Grace" and belt it big with "Climb a Higher Mountain." The energy behind her delivery is contagious. You want to stand up and sing along. And do so with purpose, fighting comfort in the words of faith, hope, courage, and redemption—hallmarks of Aretha's life.

For a woman so regal her love life was anything but. She had her first child at age twelve and another by another man when she was 14. One of her husbands was a pimp and hustler. She did not become bitter; she channeled her experience into her music, singing for every woman who had suffered at the hands of a man as well as for anyone who felt the weight of oppression due to race, class, or income.

Aretha was given a send-off fit for a queen. Entertainers including

Gladys Knight, Cicely Tyson, Ariana Grande, Chaka Khan, Smokey Robinson, and Stevie Wonder performed. Her eulogists were those who knew her music and her spirit.

Reverend Al Sharpton said, "We watched Aretha bear her cross down here. She had to sing with a broken heart. She had to work when she didn't get paid. She was a black woman in a white man's world. She bore her cross . . . She was a civil rights activist when it wasn't popular . . . She gave us pride, and she gave us a regal bar to reach . . . We don't all agree on everything. But we agree on Aretha."

President Obama, in a letter read at her funeral, said, "Aretha's work reflected the very best of the American story, in all of its hope and heart, its boldness and its unmistakable beauty." And President Clinton said, "This woman got us all in the seats today not because of her music, but because she lived with courage. Not without fear but overcoming her fears. She lived with faith—not without failure but overcoming her failures. She lived with power —not without weakness but overcoming her weaknesses. I just love her."

Those three comments, taken from the many thousands of words spoken about her passing, attest to Aretha's ability to connect with others. She demonstrated courage and righteous actions. She was kind and generous, and she had the ability to connect with millions through her music. Her life did not go as it always did on stage—powerful, enthralling, and radiant. But she lived large and, in the process, made the world better for others.

Aretha's anthem—oddly in a way since she was a prolific song-writer—was a song she did not write, "Respect," by Otis Redding. But she certainly made it her own and in doing so, set a plank in the floor for women to stand up as equal to men especially when, as in Aretha's case, they had been so long dismissed, or worse, abused. Women heard Aretha's message and it lives on. *Rolling Stone* maga-zine put Aretha on the top of its list of 100 greatest singers—women and men. "Aretha is a gift from God," singer Mary J. Blige told the magazine, "When it comes to expressing yourself through song, there is no one who can touch her. She is the reason why women want to sing." And—may we add—why we all want to listen—courage, strength and grace all resonant within one beautiful voice.[3]

Grace in Action

We can think of grace as spiritual but to my way of thinking it only works when it is put into action. If we take a look at the key virtues that make humans *human*, we can come down to a handful of virtues that make us uniquely human. These include the capacity to love. Animals can have love for their offspring and even show emotion when their young are taken from them. Some animals will even put themselves in danger, even risking death, to protect their young.

So too will humans, but humans extend the protection and sacrifice to those not related to them. We see this in all kinds of organizations from sports teams to first responders. The needs of the team outweigh the wants of a few. Each member of a team feels a sense of loyalty to another.

Trust is fundamental to human survival. Without an ability to discern real from unreal, people are adrift. While there can be interpretations, there is only a single truth. To deny truth is to deny fact; and therefore, to deny humanity. Courage emboldens individuals. As many have said, courage is not the absence of fear; it is the management of it. Courage is rooted in the strength of conviction and seeking to do what is right in the face of danger.

Nowhere is courage more vivid than within service personnel, those who put their lives at risk for our safety. A fundamental building block of organization success is cohesion. The organizational mission is fulfilled through men and women working together for a greater cause. They sacrifice for the mission, and sometimes they give their lives for it. Love for their fellow service person is the bond that binds units together. Sacrifice for a colleague, as well as for the mission, becomes an expression of love.

Love, sacrifice, truth, and courage—I believe—are virtues made actionable by grace. We may be disposed to do what is right; grace gives us the impetus to act upon doing it. Grace then becomes the inspiration for treating individuals with generosity, respect, and compassion. It manifests itself as action in the name of others and it energizes us to act upon our beliefs.

Taken collectively these virtues imply an obligation to do better—to serve others. For some, it comes naturally. Others need prodding. Service takes many forms. Love of fellow man compels some to pursue careers in the healing arts or social service. But there is space for love in any endeavor. Each of us can find the wherewithal to demonstrate kindness, not the random but intended. Kindness is a gift of self to another. Not presents, but presence. In short, being there with grace.

Inherent in Many Faiths

While grace is most commonly associated with Christianity—do a search for the topic and most resources are Christian-centric—the concept has roots in the other two Abrahamic faiths: Judaism and Islam.

Judaism, of course, predates Christianity and the notion of grace is found in the Hebrew Bible. In Exodus (xxxiv. 6) we read "The Lord, the Lord God, merciful and gracious, long-suffering, and abundant in goodness in truth." While the sense of moral justice and righteousness is prevalent in the Hebrew Bible, as authors Kaufman Kohler and M.M. Eichler note, grace parallels justice. Furthermore, the Lord grants grace not simply to Jews but also non-Jews. The caveat being there must be repentance. By contrast, in Christian thought, grace is granted, not earned.

There is also the notion of divine grace being viewed as mercy and compassion, which Kohler and Eichler write, comes from the Lord's understanding of "human weakness" as well as the need to maintain the spiritual covenant with the faithful. The Talmud, the collection of interpretive works by Jewish scholars, also seconds the idea of mercy and righteousness. Perhaps Rabbi Hillel, a 1st Century BC Jewish scholar, put it best when he said, "That which is despicable to you, do not do to your fellow, this is the whole Torah, and the rest is commentary, go and learn it." In other words, do what is good.[4]

Islam, which sprang up seven centuries after Christ, also embraces grace. Like Christianity, Islam is a faith based upon doing. It is not enough to have faith in Allah; you must practice that faith. Practice comes from the dictates in the Koran to do "good works." Allah, it can be said, grants grace to man to have faith and in turn perform acts of goodness that benefit others. For example, as J. Hashmi notes, Islam promotes charitable giving not for the benefit of self-glory but for the generosity of spirit to help others.[5]

Buddhism, too, has a concept of grace. While Buddhism is rooted in the quest for enlightenment, one can only attain such perfection if one is kind and gracious to others. Donald Altman, an author who has studied and practiced Buddhism, quotes the Dalai Lama who said, "The blessing must come from within, from one's mental attitude." As Altman writes, "If you want to give anything away, be it your love, money, time, forgiveness, regrets, sympathy, commitment, blessings . . . you must first manifest it." Inherent in those words is the practice of grace, sincerity giving back by sincere sentiment.[6]

Grace in Practice

Grace, too, particularly in the Christian tradition, is good for our transgressions. None of us is perfect and no matter what our intentions, each and every one of us will fall short of our expectations of doing good. We disrespect others. We may act with animus, even hate. We may be mean and selfish. We are human.

Yet we are capable of forgiveness. People of faith would label it as acting with the grace of God. But it might be more accurate to say that we act upon—as Lincoln might say—the better angels of our nature.

Grace, then, is within us. We can both seek forgiveness as well as forgive. In the first instance, we are open to the truth—that we have wronged others. We have acted improperly. Words of apology are expected but they are not enough. We must be willing to make amends for our transgressions, to heal those whom we have hurt. Failure to do so dooms us to a life without grace.

To forgive others has been called divine because we are putting aside our hurt in order to enable another to heal. It can be very hard to do. We are surrendering our "upper hand" to extend a "helping hand" to one who has asked us for forgiveness. Inherent in the ability to forgive is another key virtue—humility. You can define humility as the recognition that you are not infallible or sovereign. You are a composed of strengths as well as weaknesses. Understanding that duality is essential to maintaining a humble outlook on life.

Grace offers redemption to us all. It gives steel to our spines as well as humility to our souls. We recognize our fallibility. And from the recognition comes not weakness but hope, the sense that while we are not perfect, we are not weak, nor evil. We are human. We are people with grace . . . to love, to do, to be strong, to fail. . . and mostly to live the best version of ourselves.

In a eulogy for the Reverend Clementa Pickney, pastor of Grace Emanuel African Methodist Episcopal Church in Charlotte, South Carolina, President Barack Obama described how he saw the concept of grace. Reverend Pickney, along with eight fellow parishioners, had been gunned down in the church by a lone white gunman whom they had invited into their study group. The gunman's motive was to spark a racial uprising. What he got in return was a lesson in grace.

"According to the Christian tradition, grace is not earned," Obama said. "As a nation, out of this terrible tragedy, God has visited grace upon us, for he has allowed us to see where we've been blind. He has given us the chance, where we've been lost, to find our best selves. We may not have earned it, this grace, with our rancor and complacency, and short-sightedness and fear of each other—but we got it all the same. He gave it to us anyway. He's once more given us grace. But it is up to us now to make the most of it, to receive it with gratitude, and to prove ourselves worthy of this gift."

Later in his eulogy, Obama began to sing the hymn "Amazing Grace." The president concluded with an admonition that our nation should "find ourselves worthy of that precious and extraordinary gift" of grace. In that eulogy, the president invoked both a religious and secular tradition. Grace is given by God; it is not earned. As such it is therefore incumbent upon us to use it wisely. That message applies not simply to the faithful but to anyone who seeks to do better for others. It is grace in action.

Grace as Courtesy

"I can take that to the front desk if you would like," said the young sales assistant.

Ordinarily, such assistance would not warrant mentioning, except this situation was far from ordinary. The store—Babies R Us—was slated to close the following day, and my wife and I were shopping for last-minute bargains for our daughter who was soon to deliver our first grandchild. This store was frankly the last place on earth I wanted to be on a sunny spring afternoon, especially since I expected to be fighting hordes of shoppers and a surly sales staff.

Nothing could be further from the truth. The store was more barren than crowded, so empty a work crew was already dismantling the shelving, no doubt preparing the "big box shell" for the next tenant. When we paid for the item—a baby stroller with more amenities than my car's interior—the twenty-something clerk was smiling and gracious. She casually mentioned that she had grown up shopping at the parent company, Toys R Us, and in fact had given up a job to work at this store. When she made that decision, she likely did not know the chain had been regarded as a "dead store standing" for years.

Sad as the situation may be, it is worse for people who lose their jobs. As we exited the store, my wife expressed her condolences and wished the clerk good luck. The clerks were bravely shouldering on, no tears from them. There would be little to no severance pay but the clerks we encountered were polite, courteous, and even cheerful. More positively than I would be if I were losing my job!

And that's the point. These good folks were giving me a lesson in grace. They had a job to do, and they weren't about to exact revenge on customers. They exemplified something Aristotle noted a couple of millennia ago: "The ideal man bears the accidents of life with dignity and grace, making the best of circumstances." In doing so, the store clerks reminded us that while adversity is seldom planned, our reaction to it could be. Inner strength comes from having faced challenges in the past and persevering. While my wife and I got a real bargain, I got more than a piece of merchandise. I received a lesson in the power of grace. I am the lucky one![7]

Grace as Bravery

Grace becomes most evident with its absence. James Blake was standing outside a Manhattan hotel in September 2015 when he suddenly found himself tackled to the ground, handcuffed, and surrounded by five New York City policemen. As it turns out Blake fit the profile of a suspect wanted for credit card fraud. The only thing Blake, once the No. 4 ranked tennis player in the world, had in common with the criminal was his color. Both were black.

Blake was content to let the matter slip until he spoke to his wife and began thinking about what about all the other folks who are treated unjustly by police but do not have the means to fight back. Blake sued. Not for money, however. After two years of negotiation, the City of New York agreed to fund three consecutive two-year fellowships for victim-rights lawyers.

Blake tells the story in his book, *Ways of Grace: Stories of Activism, Adversity and How Sports Can Bring Us Together.* The book tells the story of activists who stood up for what they believed even when it cost them personally. Among those profiled are Arthur Ashe, Muhammad Ali, and Nelson Mandela. Of these Ashe, a Wimbledon, Australian and US Open champion, exemplifies what it means to live your values. Ashe battled discrimination throughout his career. And when his career was over, and he had been stricken with AIDS via a blood transfusion, Ashe continued fighting for the rights of Haitians and others. (Blake regards Ashe as a role model and says Ashe's memoir, *Days of Grace*, inspired him to write *Ways of Grace*.)[8]

Inspiring as these stories are, they exemplify the concept of grace. For believers, grace is both the knowledge of living in the spirit of a higher power. For laymen, grace is the sense of self that enables one to maintain equilibrium in the face of hardship. Grace for both is putting what you believe into practice for the betterment of others. And for that reason, it resonates strongly with leaders.

Leaders who demonstrate grace are those who are first and foremost comfortable in their own skins. They know themselves warts and all. They shore up shortcomings with people who can do tasks with better fluency. At the same time, such individuals do not shirk responsibility; they use it as a means to accomplish good things for the team. Adversity often brings out the best in such people. Grace in all of its dimensions, most of all courage, is something that enriches a leader's perspective making him or her at once admirable as well as accessible.

Grace as a Gift

Grace comes to us in different ways and different forms. Even as genius—from where does genius come? That is a question that anyone who looks at those who have made a difference in science, as well as the arts, asks when they encounter someone who, at a very young age, demonstrates prodigious talent. The operative word being "prodigy."

Alma Deutscher is one example. Born in 2005 to parents, who are university professors by trade and amateur musicians by avocation, Alma is an accomplished composer. "[Music] is her first language," says Robert Gierdingen, a professor of music at Northwestern in Chicago, speaking on CBS's *60 Minutes*. "She speaks the Mozart style. She speaks the style of Mendelssohn as if she were a native speaker. She's batting in the big leagues."

Alma, who was introduced to music at age 3 and taught to read music by her father Guy, is not thinking of history.

"It's really very normal to me to go around—walk around and having melodies popping into my head. It's the most normal thing in the world," she says. "For me, it's strange to walk around and not to have melodies popping into my head."

Although she is a young teen, her musical voices are eclectic. As she told Scott Pelley on CBS *60 Minutes*, "I have lots of composers. And sometimes when I'm stuck with something, when I'm composing, I go to them and ask them for advice. And quite often, they come up with very interesting things." One composer, whom she labels Antonin Yellowsink, provides her with a window into darker themes.

Alma's music—two operas as well as several concertos to date—resonates with depth. And there is a reason. "Lots of people think that the difficult part of composing is to get the ideas, but actually that just comes to me," she said at Google Zeitgeist. "The difficult bit is then to sit down with that idea, to develop it, to combine it with other ideas in a coherent way because it's very easy to throw a soup of lots of ideas which don't make any sense together. But to sit down and develop and combine it, and afterwards to tweak it and to polish it—that takes ages," she added.

Her parents live in the country and provide for Alma and her younger sister's homeschooling. The two of them also have a circle of friends, but for Alma music is a dominant theme. She can compose for up to five hours in a day. She receives tutelage from various professors who seem determined not to overwhelm her but nurture her talent. Her father, a renowned university linguist, told Israeli newspaper, Haaretz, that his daughter has a deep understanding of harmony, something he noticed when she was playing a piece by Hayden. She knew what the composer was doing because she understood how he was creating harmonic progressions.

What do the critics think of Alma? Heather MacDonald writes in *The New Criterion*: "A twelve-year-old British girl has written an opera of astounding wit, craft, and musical beauty. . . Deutscher's most impressive accomplishment is her mastery of the classical tradition's rich resources for expressing dramatic conflict." James Sohre of *Opera Today* gushes, "A young talent's sensational burst to prominence, and a buoyant production of the highest professional standard combined to make this the once-in-a-lifetime opera-going event that had audiences standing and cheering." Elizabeth Grice of *The Daily Telegraph* notes, "Cinderella proves that Deutscher is an extraordinary talent. Prodigy is a much-misused term, but the maturity of her composition would suggest that, for once, it is not mere hyperbole. That a young girl could have the mental energy to compose a two-hour opera and take credit for its full orchestration is staggering; that the end result is a lively, coherent piece of comic opera is exceptional."

Not only does Alma compose she plays. Dr. Wilhelm Sinkovicz writes in *Die Presse*: "Alma Deutscher's music, which she presents on the piano with full commitment and with palpable pleasure, is full of extraordinarily original ideas and genuine surprises so that any suspicion that a good arranger could have helped out is immediately extinguished . . . What dear god may still be planning with this girl?"

Conductor Simon Rattle told *The Guardian* newspaper that he was "absolutely bowled over" by her. Rattle told the BBC that Deutscher was "a force of nature," and said: "I don't know that I've come across anyone of that age with quite such an astonishing range of gifts. It's natural for her, it's play." Two noted conductors, Daniel Barenboim and Zubin Mehta also believe deeply in her talent and her genius. Speaking on Austrian television, Mehta called her "one of the greatest talents of today."

While a comparison to Mozart is often made, Alma would prefer to speak for herself musically and personally. "I don't really want to be a little Mozart because then I would just compose what he has composed already. That would be boring. I want to be Alma, a little Alma."[9] The beauty of grace is that while its ways can be mysterious, its impact is transformative.

Grace as Beauty

Alma's gift, like that of Aretha Franklin's, personifies another kind of grace: *beauty*. Look closely at a Monet painting—say the water lilies from Giverny—and you will see the shards of paint strokes that capture dappled blue and purple splashes of sunlight. Gaze too at photographs by the legendary Ansel Adams. His landscapes captured the beauty of the West in infinite shades of black and white. Watch the gliding Fred Astaire and Ginger Rogers whose duets graced their way across the silver screen and in the process endeared themselves to romantics ever since. Or witness the grace in the sweeping moves of ballerinas as they skate across the stage, their feet pitter-pattering rapidly on point. Such grace is the result of years of training as well as graceful interpretation.

One creative genius who embodied a sense of grace not simply in his work but also in his demeanor was Leonardo da Vinci. Biographer Walter Isaacson says that Leonardo was always very careful in his dress and worked to project a lively demeanor. One influence on Leonardo's behavior, Isaacson believes, was the polymath Leon Battista Alberti, himself a student of the great architect Franco Brunelleschi of Florence. Alberti, who was an engineer and essayist as well as priest, wrote, "One must apply the greatest artistry in three things: walking in the city, riding a horse, and speaking, for in each of these one must try to please everyone." Alberti himself was described by one biographer as "an avatar of every word or movement." Those are words that the young Leonardo who first made his reputation in Florence, the city that established the Renaissance, took to heart, and put into practice.[10]

And closer to our own time there is the suave and debonair Cary Grant—has such a movie star ever looked so stylish, as well as having a heck of a good time, on screen? It is in Grant, who learned his trade as a vaudevillian in England before coming to America, that we see the meld of elegant form combined with masculine grace. He can dance, as well as tumble, in time to the music. He can woo a heroine with a wink or smile, or in his dramatic roles, project confident masculinity that personifies courage and fortitude. Grant, of course, projects this image; that was his craft. But I choose that image as an example of what it means to move with grace, yet at the same time maintain a sense of awareness as well as self-deprecation.

In graceful movement, there is a sense of centeredness or a person who knows him or herself well. There is grace in self-awareness in both stillness and motion.

Grace as Graciousness

Being grateful for what is around us is another form of grace, and sometimes we see such appreciation in the lives of people better known than ourselves. One such person is Paul McCartney. In a blog post,

Father James Martin, S.J., editor of *America Magazine*, expressed his delight in seeing the video of the car trip James Corden and Paul McCartney took around Paul's native Liverpool. In the video, we see Paul in a shop, a park, and even in the house in which he grew up. He is also crooning along with Corden in the front seat of the car. Paul is charming and gracious and is good spirits. [The video is part of Corden's "Carpool Karaoke" series.]

Throughout the years, critics and commentators alike have noted that Paul was, as were the Beatles themselves, very much a creature of his hometown. "Penny Lane" and "Strawberry Fields," to name two, were songs about their daily haunts. You could take the Beatles out of Liverpool, but you could never take Liverpool out of them. What captures Fr. Martin's attention is Paul's sense of grace— through expressions of recognition on people's faces, Paul speaks of how he practiced in the bathroom because the acoustics were best. And in the pub, Paul took the stage with his band for a five-song set. The audience, totally unexpectant of such a treat, was in awe.

Fr. Martin also cites McCartney's innate humility. His life is less about his personality than the music he has created. Corden, a talented comedian, does his best to bring out Paul as a human being doing so in ways that make him as well as us laugh. "It is the human connection," Fr. Martin writes. The video, as a whole, "reveals how one person's living out of his or her vocation can tie so many people together. And it is deeply spiritual as well in that it shows us how the spirit can work in such beautiful, touching and unexpected ways. In such grace-filled ways."[11]

GRACE PLAYS TO ASPIRATION OF FOLLOWERS. WE WANT TO EMULATE THOSE WE ADMIRE, AND WE SEEK TO FOLLOW THEIR EXAMPLE.

Grace: What the Leaders Say

Grace is a positive force for good in our lives. How you define it—as well as how you practice it—is open to interpretation. For that reason, I asked a number of men and women whose examples of grace are evident in their work as leaders to explain what grace means to them. Here's a sampling of what they told me about how they view grace. [Their comments will be found at the end of every chapter.]

***

Grace is a "given." For that reason, Sally Helgesen believes that "exhibiting grace means stepping up and doing something that the other person didn't necessarily merit or earn."

Chris Lowney agrees, adding, "Grace is something that allows us to accomplish what we're supposed to accomplish here on earth as humans. And I happen to think that grace is a gift that we can't totally give ourselves, but it comes from outside us to some extent."

Grace for Christine Porath means "dignity and also treating others with respect, but mainly reacting with dignity to even tough situations. And I think in terms of people, to honor or dignify someone."

To Scott Moorehead, "Grace is just an inner peace and the ability to forgive and to be positive and to allow for progress, internally, externally, and all around."

"Grace is a state of being that people inhabit," says Alaina Love. "And when they inhabit that state of being, there's a centeredness that I see in them." They know themselves and they are "comfortable in their own skin." Such individuals "exhibit no overt need to compete in the sense of I'm better than you because they are so comfortable in who they are. And they carry themselves with a sense of this world being a very large place and all of us being, somehow, in this very large blue ball spinning in space, being connected to one another."

Skip Prichard agrees. "I think someone who embodies elegance and class, and someone with grace does have a default of love, does have a default of caring for others."

"Grace comes down, really, to self-control," says Mike McKinney. "Grace isn't possible if you're stuck in a mire of ego and self-absorption. And I think when grace is understood this way, we see that it widens and deepens our understanding and expands our possibilities because a lack of grace makes us small really."

Toward that end, Alan Mulally believes in the power of grace. As he says, "You're helping. You're supporting, and that just builds on generosity. It builds on respect. It builds on action and compassion, and you bring your best self and your best energy."

Dave Johnson echoes the concept of grace as energy, as well as flow. "I can feel it, it's always there, it's always available; I don't always notice it. So, for me, grace is a beautiful word that conjures up the idea or the notion of the flow of movement or energy between me as a human being and others, or the created world."

For Stephen M.R. Covey, grace is the ability to "believe in someone. To take a chance on someone. To extend trust to someone. Also, to extend generosity to someone."

Tim Sanders says, "Grace allows us to levitate above the emotional fray . . . I find grace as an attribute that a human being, not God gives us, but as a human being possesses to be quite similar to, say, emotional intelligence where there's a real balancing act involved."

***

Think about these questions:

- What does grace mean to you?

- What role does kindness play in the life around us?

- How does a lack of grace affect our world?

- How can we learn to live with grace in order to make the world better?

- What does it take to exert bravery?

- Think of an example when you were wronged. Did you forgive the transgressor? If not, would you do it differently now?

- What link can you draw between genius and grace?

Graceful Leadership Steps

Grace – *catalyzing what is good to make things better*

- Think positively about yourself as a means of doing positively for others.

- Look for ways to be kind to others. Train yourself to expect nothing in return.

- Find grace and beauty in what you typically overlook because you are too busy.

- Withhold judgment before you understand others.

- Know that the search for motive can be an excuse for finding blame.

- Determine the needs of others as a means of discovering purpose for yourself.

- Look to promote what is good and dispense with what is harmful.

- Discover your sources of inspiration: why do they mean so much to you?

- Find inspiration in the determination of others as a means of inspiring yourself to action.

Chapter 2

"Give what you have. To someone, it may be better than
you dare to think."

— Henry Wadsworth Longfellow

Generosity

G is for generosity, *the will to do something more.*

Generosity is the capacity—as George Bernard Shaw said—to question
life's purpose. "There are those that look at things the way they are,
and ask why? I dream of things that never were, and ask why not?"
Standing still is good for statues but not for people. Those who aspire
to generosity look at the status quo as a building block to creating some-
thing better.

Making the World Better for Children and Their Parents

Fred Rogers, who died in 2003, was an ordained Presbyterian
minister whose ministry was television. He never preached the
Gospel over the airwaves; he practiced it. Salvation for Fred Rogers
was not souls for God but people who practiced the Golden Rule.
The secret, if there was one, was that the Fred Rogers you saw on
television was the same Fred Rogers you would meet in person.

He was affable, approachable, and accessible. He spoke to children as people, not as stuffed toys. His show spanned decades of social change that saw America become a more tolerant culture as well as one equally riven by debate over issues related to civil, human, and women's rights.

A 2018 documentary, *Won't You Be My Neighbor?* has stirred memories of those who watched the show as children as well as those parents whose children watched it. Originally his show for children began in Toronto for the Canadian Broadcasting Network (CBC) in 1963. It moved to WQED in Pittsburgh in 1968 as *Mister Roger's Neighborhood* and within a few years went national on the Public Broadcasting System (PBS) where it ran until August 2001. The show's audience was comprised primarily of preschoolers, but its influence reached all ages.

While Rogers himself was kind and gentle in person, he was no pushover. When PBS canceled his show, there was an uproar, especially from parents of children who watched it. Rogers himself testified to Congress about the intention of his show as well as the impact it was having on children who watched it. PBS relented and put the show back on the air.

In the documentary, we see clips of how Fred Rogers explained social issues to children. In one episode about integration, Rogers put his feet into a kiddie pool right next to those of a black child. After the killing of Robert Kennedy, he did a program explaining "assassination" and what it meant. He also tackled divorce and many other issues affecting children. He was a puppeteer and, along with his wife Joanne, created a host of characters that could be used to educate as well as entertain. He also sang and played piano. His shows featured children with disabilities, demonstrating that difference in physicality did not preclude interaction.

Once Rogers went to see a 14-year old boy stricken with cerebral palsy. The boy was very upset with his condition and when he first met with Rogers, he had something of a meltdown. Rogers asked him for a favor to which, of course, the boy readily agreed. Rogers asked the boy to pray for him. The request was not intended as reverse psychology, that is, making the boy feel important. It was more basic than that. As Fred explained to journalist Tom Junod, who wrote a profile of Rogers for *Esquire* magazine, "Oh, heavens no, Tom! I didn't ask him for his prayers for *him*; I asked for me. I asked him because I think that anyone who has gone through challenges like that must be very close to God. I asked him because I wanted his *intercession*."

That story illustrates with clarity the kind of person Fred Rogers was—humble as well as vulnerable. Those two qualities were essential to his appeal because he was able to connect with so many people in such a genuine way. And do it over the airwaves. Sincerity sells, as the old advertising adage goes, but with Rogers, it was a sincerity rooted in his faith and its practice of looking at children—and the rest of us—as people who, like him, respond to warmth, friendship, and kindness.[12]

Love as Sharing

Another word to describe Fred Rogers' message is love, a word often associated with grace. In fact, many see the concept as one and the same. While I don't disagree, I prefer to think of love as the spirit behind the notion of grace as a catalyst. That is, we act on grace because we love our fellow humans and want to do right by them. We can define love in the same way we define grace—as respect and compassion—focused on doing the greater good. Love can be thought of as brotherhood, the bond that holds one to another. Two men, regarded as role models in their respective fields, considered love in this way. They are Vince Lombardi and David Hackworth.

Lombardi, the tough coach with a barking voice and gruff demeanor, was a popular public speaker. That's what winning five NFL titles, including the first two Super Bowls, will do to public demand. One of the themes of his talk was love. For Lombardi, love was rooted in "loyalty." He believed in teamwork as "the love one man has for another, and one who respects the dignity of another." Love for Lombardi was also "charity." Speaking ill of a teammate or failing to be charitable, according to Lombardi, disqualified one from being considered a leader. He called love "heart power" and viewed it as "strength."

David Maraniss, in his biography of Lombardi, notes that the man himself fell short on fulfilling love, certainly in ways he treated his teams, sometimes pitting one player against another. He also was not a perfect boss. Yet no one doubted his sincerity. Lombardi believed in what he said, even if he fell short personally. Lombardi articulated the meaning of love.[13]

David Hackworth put love into practice. As a veteran of three tours in Vietnam, Colonel Hackworth was the Army's most decorated soldier having served also in World War II and Korea. While in Vietnam, he "walked perimeter alongside his men," most of who were ill-trained draftees until they came under his command. He even made it his duty to inspect the feet of each of his soldiers to ensure they did not get a fungal infection. "When a leader gets down on his knees and touches his men's feet," Hack said, "it delivers a clear message: That the commander cares." Hack saw himself as their caretaker, making certain as many as possible would get home safe.[14]

These two men, Lombardi and Hackworth, embody what it means to care for another. Each held himself to a standard of service to another. Love, therefore, is service. It is shaped from a consideration of others that obliges the one who loves to care for others. You don't have to like other people—though that certainly helps—you need to treat them with the dignity that human beings deserve.

When it comes to love, we all fall short. There are some folks I know who embody what it means to love unconditionally. They exemplify love as service. They radiate a kind of joy that only comes from serving others. They do not seem bothered by the irritations of everyday life. They are focused on meeting the needs of others. That is love.

LeBron Love

For some celebrities, giving to charity is part of the job, showing "the love" as some might say. And frankly, they treat it like a job. They show up at a charity event, have their picture taken, stroke a check, and smile for the cameras again. They take selfies and then make a hasty exit. And there is nothing really wrong with that. The charity receives the publicity it needs to help raise money for its worthy cause.

Sad to say that when celebrities really give their time and effort, our first reaction is to dismiss their efforts as a gesture. So, it is refreshing to look at what LeBron James is doing with his millions. King James, as he has been known since his school days on the basketball courts of Akron, Ohio, is a phenomenon. Like many kids in his neighbor, he grew up poor and never had a relationship with his father. He played for and attended St. Vincent-St. Mary high school in Akron, and it was there that he learned two things: one, how to lead a basketball team; two, how to live your values.

At eighteen, he signed with the Cleveland Cavaliers and became an instant celebrity, in part due to his prodigious talent and a 100 million dollar contract with Nike. LeBron has won three NBA titles, two with the Miami Heat and one with the Cavaliers. He appeared in a record eight consecutive NBA Final series. Far too many athletes who achieve fame and fortune early end up in a bad place—broken and broke. Not LeBron. Throughout his entire career, he has been an exemplar of how to conduct oneself on the public stage. His focus off the court is on his wife and family as well as ventures into entertainment, business, and philanthropy.

In the summer of 2018, LeBron helped launch the "I Promise" public school which teaches the STEM (Science, Technology,

Engineering and Math) curriculum. It also provides support and encouragement for the development of the whole child academically, emotionally, and socially. Students who attend are considered "at risk," many of whom are one or two years behind in reading levels. These students also experience the hard side of life and "I Promise" provides what it calls "wraparound" services with job and family services, a GED program, and even a food pantry. At LeBron's insistence each kid receives a bicycle, something he used as a kid to avoid trouble. Students who graduate will be offered free tuition at the University of Akron. The school, together with scholarships to the University of Akron, is supported by the LeBron James Family Foundation.

The "I Promise" name comes from the commitment that students make to the school, promising to do everything from attending and listening to asking questions as well as being respectful, healthful, and helpful. As the school's website says, "And above all (I Promise) to finish school." In a nutshell, this school is promoting the concepts of grace that emerge from its benefactor's commitment to give back to the community. "We want every kid that walks through this school to be inspired, to come. . . away with something, something where they can give back," James told CNN's Don Lemon. "For kids, in general, all they want to know is that someone cares. And when they walk through that door, I hope they know that someone cares."[15]

Abraham Lincoln once said, "I like to see a man proud of the place in which he lives. I like to see a man live so that his place will be proud of him." LeBron is that man. He has played for three teams in three different cities, but as he says, "Know, no matter if I'm playing in Los Angeles or not, Akron, Ohio, is always home for me. Always."[16]

Generosity of Mentorship

Generosity is the giving of oneself to another. It also happens to be a good description of mentorship. As the saying goes: *Want to make a difference in someone's life? Become a mentor.* This concept was driven home to me a few years ago when I attended a going-away party for a colleague of my wife, a university health care executive. The man being feted was a physician and during the party, it came time for colleagues to comment. What resonated most with me were comments about this physician's ability to connect with others as a teacher and mentor.

Mentorship is the investment of self in others without an expectation of return. The mentor believes in the character and ability of another person and is willing to help that individual, typically someone much younger but not always, achieve his/her best. Mentorship is grounded in disinterest. That is, the relationship is not one of personal gain.[17]

Mentoring uses coaching techniques such as inquiry in order to discover an individual's character and abilities as well as areas of potential growth. Mentors, like coaches, challenge assumptions and help individuals learn more about themselves in order to become more successful. Mentors typically work in the same disciplines, so they often teach their junior colleagues much like professor/pupil.

Just as executive coaching has gained currency within the corporate world, so too has mentorship. And it makes good sense. The knowledge economy demands that individuals receive opportunities to grow into greater consciousness with grace just as they gain insight into their discipline. Mentorship provides an avenue for individualized teaching as well as development. Mentors do matter, and in the process, feel enriched by the knowledge that they have enabled someone else to benefit from their personal commitment.

Such an approach is especially appreciated by Millennials, the 73 million or so individuals born between 1980 and 1996. According to "What Millennials Want from Work and Life," a new study by the Gallup Organization, young employees seek purpose as well as development that leverages their strengths so they can become better at what they do. These are things mentors can deliver, benefitting both employees and their employers.

Three University of Michigan physicians, Jennifer Waljee,

Vineet Chopra, and Sanjay Saint designed a chart "Mentoring Millennials: Myths, Truths and Best Practices" that delineates skills that mentors can use to connect more effectively with those they mentor. Depicted in the chart are stereotypes associated with millennials. These include impatience, entitlement, laziness, narcissism, overly social, and needy. These stereotypes emerge from the mismatch from what the mentor observes and what the millennial expects.

For example, impatience—what a mentor observes—stems from being accustomed to rapid information flow—what a Millennial expects. Likewise, entitlement is an outgrowth of ignoring social conventions related to hierarchy. Millennials do exhibit a high degree of purpose and organizational mission; if they don't find it, they disengage from the work. Their desire for rapid advancement is fueled by their sense of vision and their capabilities. They are focused on big issues that affect the world, and they want to engage with others.

Connecting with Millennials, as the authors point out, means finding ways to replace perceived inertia with innovation, hierarchy with autonomy, busywork with purposeful work, subordinate status with leadership, uniformity with diversity, and isolation with community. Such an approach to mentoring provides context for development, and for this reason, is biased toward understanding the Millennial rather than the Millennial understanding a more experienced professional. As a result, mentor and mentee must strike a balance of knowledge that enables the younger person to grow his or her skills as well as adapt to the organizational structure.

Just as it is important for mentors to understand younger colleagues, it is equally important —even more so—for colleagues to learn "the system." They need to adjust their expectations for what is achievable and in what time frame, as well as to accommodate the demands of hierarchy. Mentors can coach younger colleagues about how to interact with peers, work more efficiently with bosses, and position their ideas into winning proposals for future projects.

Very importantly, mentors can serve the sounding board to provide insight into how to work cooperatively and collaboratively so that you become a trusted colleague.

"The greatest good you can do for another," wrote the 19th century British Prime Minister Benjamin Disraeli, "is not just to share your riches but to reveal to him his own." Mentors enable their protégés to bring out the best in themselves. [Note: there is a silver lining for Millennials. In due time, they will be running their organizations. They will make changes accordingly, and in time they will be doing something else: mentoring the next generation of employees.][18]

Generosity in Many Forms

Mentors come from all walks of life. Even Hollywood. The theme of the film, *The Man Who Knew Infinity* is about the mathematician Srinivasa Ramanujan, who devised a number of groundbreaking mathematical theorems. But for the invitation of G.H. Hardy, a professor of mathematics at Cambridge University, Ramanujan might have remained in obscurity. In 1914, Hardy brought him to Cambridge where he could study and eventually publish his work. Ramanujan, a college dropout, lacked the fundamentals to prove his theorems; it was Hardy who pushed him, and pushed him hard, to do develop his proofs.

The film focuses on the five-plus years the two worked together as mentor and pupil. It is Hardy (played by Jeremy Irons) who takes the young Ramanujan (Dev Patel) under his wing to serve as teacher as well as protector. In the face of great resistance, Hardy champions Ramanujan's work. As the film makes abundantly clear, Hardy's colleagues were hardly enthused about having a "lowly" Indian clerk in their math department. Through Hardy's intercession, colleagues begin to recognize the greatness of Ramanujan's mind, his dogged determination, and the genius of his work. The relationship between

Hardy and Ramanujan is rooted in respect certainly, but it is the mentorship that enables Ramanujan to fulfill his destiny.

One of the best-known mentors is one whose legacy as a comedian was long and rich but his legacy as a mentor is now just coming to light after his untimely death in 2016. Garry Shandling was a groundbreaking comedian with a forty-year career who did standup as well as serving as a stand-in host for Johnny Carson in the late 1980s. He also introduced two different types of sitcoms, both of them groundbreaking. The first was *The Garry Shandling Show*, featuring zany plots that gave him the opportunity to address the camera as "himself." His second breakthrough was *The Larry Sanders Show* where he played a put-upon talk show host struggling with the demands of hosting and producing—you guessed it—a talk show.

Shandling's career as a mentor began as his career started to peak, although he was unknown to anyone outside his orbit. Now thanks to a new HBO documentary, *The Zen Diaries of Garry Shandling*, by Judd Apatow (likely his highest-profile mentee) we can see the influence of Shandling on the career and comedy of other comic performers. "I was surprised to learn how many people he was mentoring and how seriously he took it," Apatow told *The Los Angeles Times*, "He didn't stumble into helping people. It wasn't because he felt burnt out and had nothing else to do. He made a conscious choice to give back to comedy." Speaking on NPR's *Morning Edition*, Apatow said, "You know, for 25 years he was the most important mentor that I had. But in a lot of ways, he was a mystery to me." For this reason, Apatow used Shandling's own journals as the narrative thread for the documentary.

Shandling, as befits someone so creative, could be self-absorbed and highly demanding. Throughout his life, he mourned the loss of his older brother who had died of cystic fibrosis when Garry was ten. He also wrangled with his manager, the late Brad Grey, over financial matters. In addition, he fired co-star and girlfriend Linda

Doucett from *Larry Sanders* after their breakup. She sued and won a judgment.

Unlike other artists, Shandling turned his inner search for meaning into an outward hand to help others. For that reason, Shandling serves as an inspiration to other would-be mentors. Living can be sometimes messy, but that does not mean you are not able to share life lessons with others. Just as there are no perfect people, there are no perfect mentors, just imperfect people trying to give a helping hand.

At the end of the documentary, the Buddhist Ram Dass comments about "living in your heart, not in your head." Apatow tells NPR, "Garry was ultimately exploring and trying to apply to his own life—that life really is just about loving people. It is about kindness . . . What Garry was trying to do was use these diaries to constantly remind himself to reach out, to help, to mentor—to connect."

Mentorships are rich experiences for those being developed. They benefit from the expertise and wisdom of a more experienced individual. Mentors have an uncanny knack of cutting to the chase of their profession in ways that can save the less experienced person many years of frustration. How? By sharing their stories along with their knowledge, mentors can show their mentees how to polish their craft and build their reputations. They also can advise on how to function more efficiently by focusing on what's relevant to the long-term rather than expedient for the short-term.

Apatow himself is a mentor. Responsible for hits like *The 40-Year Old Virgin, This Is Life,* and *Trainwreck,* Apatow has helped women comedians such as Lena Dunham and Amy Schumer create their own comedic projects. Apatow could well be describing the mentoring process, as he reflected on Shandling's life for *The Los Angeles Times* saying, Garry "tries to figure out what's important and what's not important, he tries to give back as much as he can while he's here, and suddenly he's gone. And in a way that's everybody's journey."

Mentorships are not one-way streets. Mentors soon learn that things they took for granted—even those things learned the hard way—are of value to someone earlier in his or her career. It is richly rewarding to share yourself with someone who can benefit from your experience.

There is an entry in one of Shandling's later journals, as Apatow tells NPR, that reveals what comedy meant to him. "I should be grateful that I'm funny and for comedy, because it's a gift that I can give to people that help them deal with this long, difficult life." The very same may be said of mentorship, too. Legacy is like an annuity. It pays dividends in the actions of others. The legacy of good leaders is one that creates a prosperous and purposeful future.[19]

Generous Teaching

Mentoring has its roots in teaching. And before you can connect effectively as a teacher you need to understand the needs of your students. A friend of mine, Tim Katanski, is one such teacher. He teaches golf. Like the good teacher he is, Tim works with the talents and aspirations—as well as the limitations—of amateur golfers. Most of us are, frankly, not that good—certainly as compared to those who make a living from the game. But all of most of us do want to get better. Tim knows this and gives us advice that is based upon what we can and should do to improve.

Tim goes the extra mile for his students. Some of the men and women he coaches have some degree of physical handicap; that is, missing an eye or a limb. As Tim explained to me, before he felt was able to work with these folks, he simulated their limitation. For example, he taught himself to hit balls with one eye closed, to swing a club with one arm, and to balance on one leg while making a golf shot. Tim's reasoning was that unless he could see and feel as his pupils did, he would not be able to coach them effectively.

Tim's methodology resonates work that executive coaches do. Part of coaching requires that the ability to see the world the executive does. Coaches need to view the challenges and opportunities as their clients see them. Doing so provides a deeper sense of reality. Coaches do more than understand; they also teach. A coach can provide insights that the individual can use to see better, do better, and manage better. In other words, while we may understand their world view, we must sometimes help them shatter that perspective in favor of one that is less biased and more open-minded.

Such a perspective extends beyond the coaching world. Managers need to be in tune with the people they supervise. While few, if any, have the time to adopt the individual points of view of their direct reports, they do need to know their talents and skills as well as their desires. Doing this enables them to provide more than direction; it enables the manager to coach the individual to better performance.

I have seen this approach in action. Smart executives spend a good deal of time working to improve the performance of individual employees. For some, it means providing access to new training. For others, it requires more development time. For still others, it means giving them new responsibilities. In each case, these executives are working individually coaching them for improvement.

Their coaching, like that of Tim's, is rooted in an understanding of what the employee can do, as well as what he is capable of doing better. Expectations may be set high; so too are the systems of support. Doing this can help good performers become more prepared to achieve better results. Such coaching is time intensive because you need to make time to know your people. And it is rewarding when the individual and the team succeed together.[20]

Teaching Us to Act Generously

There is nobility to teaching. It is the sharing of knowledge from one who knows to one who wishes to know more. Good teachers do something more. They embolden us to act. In her *New Yorker* essay about her teacher and mentor, the author William Zinsser, Diana Goetsch writes, "One of the things the great teachers do is prepare you for their absence. They give you confidence, they give you your life, and, by doing so, they make themselves obsolete." A teacher's job is done when the pupil learns the subject and can demonstrate knowledge, which is assessed either through an exam or through practice. Mastery of the subject gives them the confidence to succeed. Reflecting on Goetsch's observation made me realize that truly good managers and leaders do the very same.

We see this same example in business. Most often successful executives with whom I have worked tell me about a boss who made a positive impression on them. Such a boss typically shaped the individual's career by sharing that expertise as well as sharing the wisdom necessary to master not simply the job, but a career. Such bosses were and are teachers, plain and simple. Their lessons are not held in a classroom they are held in offices, hallways, cubicles, lunchrooms, and wherever employees gather. The lessons revolve around what's happening in the business as well as what's necessary to learn in order to become more effective. So how do great bosses do this?

Invite questions. Implicit in teaching one-on-one is the notion of questioning. Curiosity is essential to learning so good managers make it known they welcome questions. Questioning reveals two important things: one, what students already know; two, what they need to know to become better.

Reveal insights. Back and forth questioning is good, but it is good for the manager to share what he or she knows. This sharing can be in the form of an explicit lesson or it can be in the form of a story. The former is good for relating technical information; the latter is better for teaching lessons about development and leadership.

Question assumptions. Teaching employees to be skeptical of easy answers is a good practice. When employees are expected to push back on what they have learned, they demonstrate that they have learned. Their challenge then is to prove their new learning. Sometimes it will affirm what already is known. Other times it will open new avenues of discussion and learning.

Critical to Goetsch's description of teaching is the notion of confidence. And this is something that mentors such as Zinsser and good managers do well. They prepare their protégés for the wider world. They impart what they can impart through their teaching but also instill within them the confidence that they can succeed. Absence, as the saying goes, makes the heart grow fonder but in the case of good teaching, it is preparation for them to succeed on their own.[21]

Acting on Generosity

Generosity is inherent to mentoring, but for some, the act of giving to others can seem daunting. They may be inclined to give, but uncertain of where to begin. One man who knows a lot about this topic is Wayne Baker, who is a professor of sociology at the University of Michigan's Ross School of Business. Assisting Wayne in this effort is his social scientist partner and wife, Cheryl Baker. Twenty years ago, Baker was looking for a way to tap into social capital as a network and create a form of reciprocity. As Baker told me in an email interview, a discussion with Cheryl sparked an idea. "Cheryl asked me to describe generalized reciprocity and I told her about the Kula Ring and how it works. From this exotic example, she created the Reciprocity Ring!" [Note: The Kula Ring, popularized by anthropologist Bronislaw Malinoski, is a form of ritualized gift exchange used by New Guinea's Trobriand Islanders.]

"Reciprocity Ring creates a context that releases that generosity," said Baker. "The Reciprocity Ring is built around asking for and giving help. It taps the collective knowledge, networks and energy of a group to meet each person's request." One student whom Baker had known when he was doing his doctoral studies at Michigan is Adam Grant. Writing in *Fast Company*, Grant, now a much-in-demand thought leader, best-selling author, and professor at the Wharton School described the Ring as the ability to tap into a network of resources facilitated by knowing someone in the Ring. As Grant puts it, "You're able to access a much wider knowledge base: *Who you know?* becomes *Who (and what) do we all know?*" Participation in the Ring makes it easy for people to "share a tip or make a call that has real benefit to others." According to Baker, the Reciprocity Ring "is a form of colleague to colleague service—just on steroids!"

Giving is not the same for everyone. "We have seen gender differences," says Baker. "Women are more likely to suffer generosity burnout. They help but don't ask for what they need, hence, burnout. Men give and ask for help." And here's where participation in the Reciprocity Ring can be advantageous. "In the Reciprocity Ring, participants are required to make a request. It helps when they know that everyone will make a request. Everyone is in the same boat."

For some asking for help can be an issue. They pride themselves on being "self-reliant." But as Baker notes you can take that too far and as a result you remain in stasis, just grinding along. Being part of a group, as in the Reciprocity Ring, makes asking for help part of the process, that is, everyone's doing it. One of the benefits of the Reciprocity Ring is that it builds upon the emotional needs people have. As Baker says, "People don't leave their emotions on the doorstep when they go to work. They might feel like they have to hide them or dampen them down, but I think in the best workplaces where people are actually thriving. They're emotional and even joyful as well."

Life is Reciprocal

Generosity can be positive to one's own emotional health. "Adam Grant and I did an interesting study," says Baker. "We measured people's positive and negative emotions prior to participating in the Reciprocity Ring and then we measured them afterwards." Baker and Grant discovered that people felt more positive emotions and fewer negaive ones after participating.

A key to making the Reciprocity Ring work is personal engagement. "It's easier to ask for what you need when you learn that making an intelligent request actually increases others' perception of your competence," says Baker. Participants learn "to use SMART criteria: specific, meaningful, action-oriented, real, time bound" to get what they want when they need it. Respectful engagement and task enablement are fundamental to the Reciprocity Ring. Baker states, "Respectful engagement is authentically listening to other people and responding to their needs, and task enabling is helping someone with what they need to get done. Whether it's an answer, a solution, advice, social support, whatever it might be."

Participation in the Reciprocity Ring stimulates generosity. "We've seen this again and again where people say, 'I don't know if I'm going to be able to help. I don't think I can help anyone.'" They say that kind of privately in the beginning, and then when they see people being really generous," they adopt the example of these folks as role models. At the same time, they realize their personal limitations. They do what they can with the resources they have.

The Reciprocity Ring focuses on personal requests and work requests. You ask for something that benefits you on a personal level. Some ask for support with a charity; others may ask for help working through personal issues. For work, people ask for insight, advice, and connections that can help the individual and the team become more effective. Creating Reciprocity Rings can occur at any organization, but now the Bakers along with Grant have created a technology platform they call "Givitas" to facilitate the giving process. What the technology encourages is quick and easy participation that can be routinized and thereby integrated into daily practice.

Technology, of course, only enables giving. The actual process of investing yourself in the life—if only for a moment—requires intention and a commitment to serve. And when it occurs, as Baker's long experience with Reciprocity Rings illustrates, it can be most satisfying and in turn enriching to others and to self. Sharing what you have with colleagues creates a more engaged workforce. It invests your purpose in the collective purpose of the enterprise—one colleague at a time. That leads to a greater sense of cooperation and collaboration —the kind that only arises when people trust one another implicitly.[22]

Generous Legacy

The mark of a good leader—as mentors know—is the impact he or she has on the people being led. Writing in the *Annals of Surgery*, Marcelo Cerulo and Dr. Pamela Lipsett quantify the effect that one surgeon, John L. Cameron M.D. of Johns Hopkins, has had on the men and women he has trained and mentored. Of the 106 surgical residents identified in the study, 84% pursued careers in academic medicine, 25% went into private practice and another 17% had careers in both fields. Over half of those in academic medicine achieved full professorships and of those in private institutions, 37% held roles of chief. Another 56% became departmental chairs or served on leadership boards.

Dr. Cameron, as the article points out, had a distinguished career in his own right as a surgeon, researcher, scholar, and administrator. The surgeons he trained speak of the "personal influence" Dr. Cameron exerted in their careers. As Cerulo and Lipsett write, "Dr. Cameron routinely personally provided advice and mentorship, and created an environment where his highly talented faculty did the same." He made certain his students had a solid plan of development and encouraged cross-training in "public health, management or basic science."

Dr. Cameron also saw to it that his surgeons received "leadership training." The authors of the study liken Dr. Cameron's example to the words of British surgeon Sir Berkeley Moynihan who said, "The chief legacy which a surgeon can bequeath is a gift of spirit. To inspire many successors with a firm belief in the high destiny of our calling . . . and to practice the knowledge so acquired with lofty purpose, high ideals and generous heart for the benefit of humanity—that is the best that a man can transmit." While Dr. Cameron has stepped down from his chairmanship, his influence persists not only in the surgeons he trained but also in the more than 1,000 surgical residents his trainees have educated.

The rigorous analysis of this article demonstrates the measurable effect that leaders can have on their followers. In the 1999 book *First, Break All the Rules,* authors Marcus Buckingham and Curt Coffman cite Gallup research noting managers who are responsible for preparing their direct-reports for higher levels of responsibility. Many of these former underlings achieved senior positions within their organizations. These managers are building the leadership corps one direct report at a time. In my experience nearly, every senior leader I know owes his or her career advancement to a boss who took them under their wing and showed them the ropes.

Leadership really comes down to example. It's not what a leader says as much as what she does. When it comes to the development of others, people remember those who helped them learn and grow their skills. They also recall, sometimes with a wince, the times when the boss called them out when they were in the wrong. Such errors were less about the quality of their work but more about how they had treated, or mistreated, colleagues. If they paid attention, they learned from their mistakes, and even better, became more adept at managing and leading others. Legacy is like an annuity. It pays dividends in the actions of others. The legacy of good leaders is one that creates a prosperous and purposeful future. [23]

GENEROSITY IS THE APPLICATION OF GOODNESS TO THOSE AROUND YOU. IT IS SERVICE TO OTHERS GIVEN IN THE SPIRIT OF HUMILITY.

Generosity – What the Leaders Say

Inherent to the concept of grace in action is generosity, a giving of self in all kinds of ways.

***

"Generosity for me is about time or talent or a giving of presence," says Dave Johnson. "It's with deep pain in life, as one goes through life's struggles that one becomes more interested, available, willing to be generous to others, to one's communities."

"We show generosity to one another by being as enthusiastic and as positive as we can be with our yes's," says Sally Helgesen, "when we have the expertise, the bandwidth, the ability to say yes to somebody."

Chris Lowney agrees that generosity is outward driven. "People who offer their time, their coaching to somebody who could benefit from it." It's "a willingness to train somebody else, the willingness to be supportive to a colleague who might be suffering or who might be the marginalized one or the outcast."

Likewise, Alaina Love believes, "We become more generous when we decide to expand our capacity for loving others. And that's a big word, and it's a big word to use in a business setting. But when you expand your capacity for love, the generosity flows from there."

Scott Moorehead integrates generosity into this business. "My desire for generosity is to be somewhat of a fire starter and to allow others the benefit to give and be generous with their time." How? By offering employees paid time off to do volunteer work.

Stephen M.R. Covey looks at generosity as the ability "to assume positive intent in others. That takes generosity of spirit to do. In any situation we start from the standpoint of saying 'My beginning point is, I assume, positive intent. There may be things here that are happening that I don't know about.'" Covey cites the example of the recently retired CEO of PepsiCo, Indira Nooyi, saying her father taught her this lesson: "Assume positive intent. You'll be amazed how that changes how you view everything."

For Tim Sanders, generosity is selfless, that is, you expect nothing in return. "I believe that you do the best when you assume, they pay it forward. When they ask you, 'What can I do to repay the favor?' You coach them on paying it forward. 'Paying it forward,' I tell people, 'that's what makes the world go around.' Doing so enables us to focus on the giving rather than the receiving."

***

Think about these questions:

- How do you define generosity?

- What could you be doing to become more generous?

- What does it mean to change the world?

- How do we demonstrate "love" as generosity?

- Think of how mentors have changed your life. How can you repay the favor?

- In what ways can you be generous to colleagues?

Graceful Leadership Steps

Generosity—*thinking big as a means of doing something good for others*

- Consider what you can do to make the world—that is, the space that you inhabit—better.

- Look for opportunities to mentor others by considering what skills you have and how you might share them with someone younger.

- Consider problems as "teachable moments," and opportunities to educate rather than excoriate.

- Find opportunities to "invest in" the lives of those most important to you.

- Read stories of women and men in history who have made their worlds better.

- Make the "hard choices" by basing your decision on what is best for the organization rather than what's best for yourself.

- Look to your community for examples of women and men making a positive difference.

Chapter 3

Civilization is a method of living, an attitude of equal respect for all men.
—Jane Addams

Respect

R is respect, *the dignity of life and work.*

Self-awareness opens the door to respect for others. Without recognizing who you are, you cannot recognize the other person. A fully self-aware person knows her faults as well as her strengths. Such awareness compels the self to acknowledge the dignity of others. In doing so we acknowledge our own humanity and its capacity for goodness.

A Life Well-Remembered

*"**He was eternally positive.** He always had a smile on his face and a song on his lips. He once told me, 'Don't ever gripe about the cards that you've been dealt. Don't worry about anyone else's cards. Just play the cards the best you can and be thankful that you get to play.'"*

That is one of the many things that Murray Howe said at the funeral of his father, hockey legend Gordie Howe, who played 26 seasons in the NHL more than any other player. Big and tough as well as graceful, Howe scored more goals and assists than anyone in his time and served as the game's greatest ambassador and one of its most beloved characters. Howe was Mr. Hockey.

There was a fad some years ago about having students write their obituaries. It is an exercise that I found a bit dry not to say a touch morbid. Better to write your eulogy. An obituary is a sum of the facts of your life; a eulogy is a hymn to how you lived your life. When your time of passing no one really cares about the facts; they want to remember you for how you made them feel, how you made them care, and how you made the world a better place. And in that regard, Murray Howe, the only Howe son not to play professional hockey—opting for a career as a physician instead—sent off his father in a fitting manner.

What so many remember about Howe off the ice was his simplicity and disarming demeanor. Here are two anecdotes of many in this vein that Murray shared:

- "There are endless superlatives that come to mind when describing my dad... Humble. A man came over for an autograph, and a woman saw him signing something, and she rushed over and said, 'Are you somebody famous?' And he said, 'No, I just used to babysit that guy.'"

- "He was prompt. He was never late for anything. To him, it was courtesy. He made it a point to show up early and chat with whomever he happened to meet. It was not surprising to find him helping the servers to set up tables at events where he was the featured speaker."

Humility was a theme of remembrances of Howe. Many of hockey's greatest were in attendance for the two-day memorial services held for Howe in Detroit. Wayne Gretzky, who broke Howe's scoring records, idolized Howe as a child, so much so that he wore No. 99 in tribute to Howe's number nine. "When I met Gordie," Gretzky told the media—echoing what he has said many times—"he was bigger, better and nicer. He was everything and more that I imagined him to be. He has a way about him, whether he was talking to my father, one of the waitresses at the diner, or the prime minister. He had a way with anybody and everybody, put everybody at ease. He was that nice. Just a really good person."

In his eulogy, Murray said Howe always deflected credit for his career to his teammates and coaches. "And he never had a bad word to say about anyone, except for referees." Howe, as Murray recalled, had a playful sense of humor. Once he whispered conspiratorially to a woman who worked at the FBI that he knew where Jimmy Hoffa was buried. When the woman wanted to know more, Howe quipped, "In the ground."

Howe's eulogy was not a recitation of hockey heroics. It was a reflection of stories that captured Gordie's life force, "as a man never looked down on those who looked up to him." That statement was how Muhammad Ali, who was buried on the same day Howe died, wanted to be remembered and serves as a fitting remembrance for both sports legends. Son Murray closed with a blessing that sums up how every father would like to be remembered. "Namaste. I humbly bow to you Dad, for your magnificent example for all of us. We will do our best to follow your lead until we meet again. Thank you."[24]

Serving Others

Gordie Howe was considered the greatest hockey player of his era yet as his passing illustrated, he never acted as the center of attention. He was humble, in part because he respected others, and thought himself no better. If you want to help, you first need to listen. That is a philosophy that Father Greg Boyle, S.J., founder of Homeboy Industries in East Los Angeles, employs. "If you're humble, you'll ask the poor, what would help you? But if you're led by hubris, then you tell the poor, here's what your problem is; here's how you fix yourself."

That's an approach that Homeboy Industries, the largest gang intervention program in the nation, employs. "Homeboy has sort of stayed humble in as much as it's listened to the formerly gang-involved and has responded at every turn." It asks the question: "what can we do that is concretely helpful?" Fr. Greg told Terry Gross on NPR's *Fresh Air*.

The minute you think you know how to help someone may also be the moment you get it wrong. Your intention is admirable, but your approach may be wrong. No one likes to be told how to get better; they want to participate in the process. That begins with a conversation, a discovery of what the other is feeling and how he or she can help in his own improvement, be it getting better at a job or recovering from addiction. Managers, too, can learn from this approach. As the boss you set direction, but it is up to individuals on the team to perform the tasks necessary to do their jobs. A manager who is always hovering, wanting to help out, is doing nothing more than hindering the individual's ability to learn. This is one reason why micromanaging is so destructive. It erodes an employee's ability to learn and grow in the job.

Maintaining a sense of humility is essential in connecting to others more realistically. For some, humility is the acknowledgement that you don't have all the answers. An emerging leader may find that concept terrifying: If I don't know what to do, who does? In reality, people around you have the answers. Humility is that openness to others. It unfolds a pathway of service to others that is rooted in self-knowledge. You know there are obstacles greater than you can overcome individually but when you surrender a part of yourself to serving the team, you belong to a community that just might surmount those obstacles.

Cultivating humility requires discipline, something effective leaders possess. Begin by reflecting on what you do well, as well as what you need help doing. Examine mistakes you have made that have resulted in your not asking for help. Identify who can help you achieve team goals. Ask for help from those who know more than you do on a given topic. And finally, listen to what they say and help them put their good ideas into practice. Knowing your shortcomings is not a limitation when you know how to listen.[25]

Humility as a Sign of Respect

One man who has lived life in respect of others and with a sense of giving back is one who lives in a modest ranch house in the town in which he was born. He flies commercial. He vacations from time to time to places around the world. He has written 33 books, a few of them on his faith and his values. He has a library and center named for him. And with good reason. He is the 39th president of the United States, Jimmy Carter.

A one-term president, Carter has set the pace for what it means to be an ex-president. Defeated soundly by Ronald Reagan in 1980, Carter returned home to Plains. He was still just 56 with plenty of life ahead of him. He was also $1 million dollars in debt since his farm had been put into a blind trust. Carter was undaunted.

Despite his finances, Carter eschewed fat speaking fees and did not serve on corporate boards. He made his living as an author and his legacy as a peacemaker. Carter spent his years—more than any other person as an ex-president —and his time mediating elections, serving as a moderator in conflicts, and championing human rights. Now that he is his nineties, his pace is slowed but he still manages to teach Sunday school in his local Baptist church. He is an evangelical Christian and one who lives his faith through his example. "I have one life and one chance to make it count for something," he wrote. "My faith demands that I do whatever I can, wherever I am, whenever I can, for as long as I can with whatever I have to try to make a difference."

Carter, along with wife Rosalyn, has been an active participant in Habitat for Humanity, building over 4300 homes in the past forty years. He was so adept at construction that when he and his wife—both in their nineties—knocked out a wall in their own home during a remodel. He has also survived cancer. Carter, however, is not an all work and no play type—he likes to fish, read, and do woodworking. Stuart Eizenstat, a former top aide and Carter biographer, told the *Washington Post*, "Plains is really part of his DNA. He carried it into the White House, and he carried it out of the White House."

His greatest triumph, and likely, his greatest disappointment, came from the Middle East. He brokered peace between Israel and Egypt by bringing Menachem Begin and Anwar Sadat together at Camp David in 1977. For twelve days he shuttled between the two men, each bitterly opposed to the other. At the end, the two shook hands and peace has lasted since. Carter's biggest disappointment was the taking of 53 American hostages by Iranian Revolutionaries in Teheran. A failed rescue attempt in 1980 cost the lives of 8 service people. The hostages were not released until the moment Reagan took office.

Carter too never lost faith in America. He is a graduate of the Naval Academy and served on the first nuclear submarine. He believes deeply in the ideals of the nation and what it means to the world. "America did not invent human rights. In a very real sense," he said, "human rights invented America." Defeat did not daunt him. Carter persevered and carved a path unlike other presidents, but one that is most important to him. "Earlier in my life I thought the things that mattered were the things that you could see, like your car, your house, your wealth, your property, your office," he wrote. "But as I've grown older I've become convinced that the things that matter most are the things that you can't see—the love you share with others, your inner purpose, your comfort with who you are."

Carter is an optimist. "I believe that anyone can be successful in life, regardless of natural talent or the environment in which we live. This is not based on measuring success by human competitiveness for wealth, possessions, influence, and fame, but adhering to God's standards of truth, justice, humility, service, compassion, forgiveness, and love." As rooted as Carter is in the reality our world, he remains a man of faith. "Spirit is like the wind," he wrote, "in that we can't see it but can see its effects, which are profound." Grace in action, perhaps.[26]

Leading with Respect for Others

President Carter lives a humble life, but that does not mean he lacks in self-esteem. He lives simply, but purposefully. Leaders of the future, former CEO Alan Mulally told me, will be those who can bring people together across disciplines. That requires the recognition of one's own limitations; no one individual knows everything required to achieve organizational success. "It's going to be people that can facilitate, bring people together around that compelling vision, strategy, and plan and having a comprehensive strategy in that relentless implementation, the process, and the behaviors" to achieve the mission, says Mulally.[27]

Such leaders readily admit they don't have all the answers; they seek the counsel of others in order to help them make key decisions. Such openness is not weakness but strength because they have the courage to admit their limitations. Such an admission is an affirmation of their courage; strong leaders are not afraid to admit mistakes. Rather they use their failures as stepping stones to greater awareness. While our culture pushes individuals to achieve and while that is good, believing in our "own pressing clippings" leads to a sense of entitlement. Humility is the anti-thesis of entitlement. It reminds us that we are not invincible, and in fact, that we are flawed as individuals. More holistically, humility opens the door to self-understanding. It enables us to recognize we need the support of others to live a full life. In leadership humble leaders are those who are not afraid to show their vulnerability.

Self-Awareness Begins with Humility

None of us is perfect and sometimes we make mistakes, so much so, that we may even doubt our own abilities. For example, Kerry Egan, a hospice chaplain, told Terry Gross on NPR's *Fresh Air*, "I don't know that I'm a great chaplain quite frankly . . . And I mean that honestly . . . 'cause I have worked with people who are great chaplains . . . I try really hard, but I fail a lot."

Egan, who is the author of a memoir, *On Living*, is committed to her chaplaincy work nonetheless. "I think it makes me a happier person because I'm constantly reminded of the strength of the human soul. I'm constantly reminded of what people can do and accomplish and get through. I am constantly reminded of love and the power of how much love people have for each other and the love that's all around us that we just don't necessarily take a moment to see."

Health care chaplains, as Egan describes them, are not affiliated with a particular faith. The job of hospital or hospice chaplain is to work with people where you find them in their life's journey. According to Egan, it's not a "preaching or teaching" role. As Egan says, "Our role [as chaplains] is to say, what is it you believe and how does that help you or not help you in this process, this process of dying, this process of letting go of the life you've loved—or maybe have not loved—and coming to some peaceful place?"

Chaplains help their clients find meaning in their work, their lives, and their relationships with others. Integral to chaplaincy is an ability to demonstrate presence, being in the moment when you are fully engaged with another individual. Chaplains must "model" presence. "You need to keep it together so that the other person can sort of fall apart," says Egan. But that's just the starting point. According to Egan, the chaplain guides the person "back to a place of peace" where they can find their bearings and restore a sense of order to their lives. [28]

And that is a lesson that each of us can demonstrate to people we know who are suffering. We can be present for others. We can abide with them in their moments of pain. Find help for them if asked, or simply spend time with them, sometimes listening but always being present.

Respect for Those in Need

One man who decided to be present is José Andrés who arrived in the United States in 1991 with $50 in his pocket. While he had no money, he had big dreams which began with something small—tapas, small portions of food common in his native Spain. Today José Andrés is a mega-star chef with more than 25 restaurants located in the most sophisticated food locales in America—Beverly Hills, South Beach, and Washington D.C. His restaurants have earned two Michelin stars.

While his food is high-end, José Andrés touches people on a basic level. As he told Anderson Cooper for CBS *60 Minutes*, "Food touches everything. Food is in our DNA. Food touches the economy. Food is science. Food is romanticism. Food is health. Food has many of the opportunities to have a better tomorrow."

Pursuing culinary stardom is not José Andrés's biggest motivator. "I am a cook. I feed the few, but I've always been super interested in feeding the many." Jose Andrés made his first outreaches to feed more in Haiti. After the 2010 earthquake devastated that island nation, he founded the World Central Kitchen. For all that he has done in Haiti, including improving the very process cooking, by enabling residents to cook with gas rather than charcoal. As a result, food becomes, in his words, "an agent of change." In 2015 José Andrés was awarded the 2015 National Humanities Medal.

As much of the good works that José Andrés did in Haiti, his achievement was but a warmup act for Puerto Rico. Immediately after Hurricane Maria hit in October 2017, World Central Kitchen moved in and began feeding up to 100,000 people a day. "Americans in Puerto Rico were hungry, and we were not delivering food quick enough," Andrés told Cooper. "And what we did is we didn't plan. We didn't meet. We began cooking, and we began delivering food to the people in need in Puerto Rico."

As noble as his effort was, bureaucracy was an obstacle. This is a theme that José Andrés continues in his book, co-written with Richard Wolffe, *We Fed an Island.* "It was already clear to me that this was a deadly serious humanitarian crisis," he writes. "It was also an untold disaster, hidden from view and lied about by our public officials. My mission was to help my fellow American citizens, and to tell their story to a world that was living in the dark." Righteous anger fuels José Andrés' desire to work for change but it does not stop him from his work. "What we did was embrace complexity every single second," Andrés writes. "Not planning, not meeting, just improvising. The old school wants you to plan, but we needed to feed the people." The work continues, World Central Kitchen has sent chefs to Hawaii, Guatemala, Indonesia, and other places where disasters have struck.

José Andrés's approach to feeding the mass is based on a grass-roots philosophy. As summarized by Tim Carman in the *Washington Post*, "Work with available local resources, whether residents or idle restaurants and schools. Give people the authority and the means to help themselves. Stimulate the local economy." Food is life for José Andrés and by sharing it—through his cooking and his volunteer outreach programs—he has transformed it into grace.[29]

Leveraging Self-Respect

José Andrés met the challenge of adversity by doing good for others. For others, adversity defines them. Ester Perel, speaking to Terry Gross on NPR's *Fresh Air* addressed her parents' experience as Holocaust survivors. Perel said the community in which she grew up in Belgium (where her parents had migrated after being liberated) was comprised of fellow survivors. She said her parents were ones who spoke about their experience. You had to be very tough and hard to survive in the camps, says Perel. The weaker ones died. Her parents suffered severe trauma but survived and were reborn. Others were not so fortunate, a part of them died in the camps—their spirit perhaps—and it was never reborn, even after liberation.

Perel has written much about the Holocaust experience and today she is a well-known psychotherapist with a practice in couples' therapy. For the past few years, she has focused on infidelity and the effect it has on relationships; her book on this subject is *The State of Affairs: Rethinking Infidelity*. An affair, of course, can destroy a marriage, but couples have a choice, either to quit the relationship or renew it. Although most often, the affair is not a life-threatening event, saving a broken marriage requires a lot of faith and determination, just as her parents did with their Holocaust experience. They did not let the trauma rob them of a future life.

Personal defeats, like broken marriages, can bring on feelings of giving up, especially if we have invested ourselves totally. For example, if we have worked hard to bring a project to fruition and it fails, there is a sense of loss. How could things have gone so wrong when you had worked so hard? If we are disciplined by our boss, we feel disappointment, even rejection. The challenge is what to do next. First, we must analyze what went wrong. Consider mistakes that were made and why they were made. Only by understanding the problem can you come to a solution.

Beyond the diagnosis, however, there is a sense of emotional loss. You put yourself into something that fizzled. Failure leads to rejection; you can lose confidence. When that happens, you feel at a loss about what to do next.

Most often with work projects we can get right back at it, but not always. Sometimes we lose our jobs. Then what? Most importantly you cannot give up on yourself. You cannot let the failure define your future. You must learn from it through analysis of your assumptions as well as your behaviors. Such study can give you lessons about how to proceed in the future.

"I've come to believe," writes motivational master Tony Robbins, "that all my past failure and frustrations were actually laying the foundation for the understandings that have created the new level of living I now enjoy." Knowing that "failure and frustrations" are part of life is fundamental to deciding to make the best of what happens next. You can shut yourself off and sulk or you can choose to do what you can to improve the situation. It requires faith in yourself, a faith in your ability to learn from the past and face the future.[30]

Making respect part of the game (of life)

Professional golfers know all about overcoming self-doubt. Someone, either in the gallery or on television, is watching every shot they take. When they hit the ball well, they look terrific; when they miss-hit it and the ball goes awry, they look ordinary. Imagine having every move you make on public view. It takes a certain strength of character to be able to perform in public, and at the same time those who do it well, very often do it by playing nice.

Professional golf may be the only sport that rates its players on being "nice when no one is looking." That's a pretty good definition of character, too. Especially when you consider PGA Tour players are expected to treat fans well, serve as "good role models," and treating the "little people" well. *[Little people includes the hundreds of people who work behind the scenes at every tournament to ensure that things go well for players as well as fans.]*

Golf Digest gives an award for being a "Good Guy." The quotes above are criteria for this award. The 2017 winner was Jordan Spieth, who by age 23 had racked up 10 wins, including two Majors. And yes, he's the same Jordan who suffered a meltdown Sunday afternoon at the 2016 Masters losing his lead after going 4-over (including two balls in the pond) on No. 12. Spieth never lost his cool.

Being nice is inherent to golf. Along with its onerous rules—which, by the way, are being loosened for 2018—players are expected to police themselves, including calling penalties on themselves for infractions no one would see. Honesty is the by-word as is treating your fellow golfers respectfully. Competition does not preclude courtesy. Arnold Palmer, the man who launched golf into the modern age on television, was unfailingly polite on the tour. He was quoted as saying that he would have won more tournaments if he had not stopped to acknowledge all the people who cheered for him as he walked up tournament fairways. No matter Arnold won 95 times worldwide, including 7 Majors. And he earned hundreds of millions, thanks to his geniality that made him an advertising sponsor's go-to guy.

True niceness is not about cashing in. I define "nice" as being available and approachable. Golfers, unlike many other professionals, are readily accessible if only for the reason that they walk every round of every tournament (at least 6-and-half miles) where the only separation from crowds is a thin rope line if there is even a rope at all. Fans know the good guys from the not-so-good ones. The ones who smile and make eye contact, and will pose for selfies or sign autographs, are fan favorites. The ones who won't, aren't. Pretty simple. [Note: I am referring to post-round behavior. It is unfair to expect a player to break concentration while playing to sign autographs, though some players will oblige.] Palmer took pride in making his autograph recognizable. "What's the point of signing something," he said, "if the person can't read it or later can't even remember who it was."

What we non-pros can learn from such behavior is how to behave in public. And this is important for leaders, especially. Why? Because leaders like golfers are always on stage, even in their off hours. For this reason, making nice is not a "nice-to-do" *(pun intended)* it's a must-do. The boss who blows off employees, tells off-color jokes, and leers at the opposite sex is not someone who is acting maturely. The boss who makes time to listen, offers encouragement to employees, and asks how you are is not a saint; he is a person who respects others. [31]

Respect in the Workplace

Louis Carter believes that respect is a key driver for workplace harmony. It operates on four levels: one, how we view ourselves; two, how we regard others; three, how we function as a team; and four, how we relate to our organization. Knowing what you can offer to others and feeling good about it enables you to be a better colleague. And in turn, when colleagues know what you can do and how you do it, they want you as a team. They value you and being valued is essential to how we want to be regarded by our team.

"Respect is a social currency," Carter, CEO of the Best Practice Institute (BPI), told me in an interview. "The more you give it, the more you get it." Louis made an analogy about the work each of us does. "We respect each other, we respect our work, we both believe in emotional connectedness, we both believe in respect in the workplace. If we didn't share, we wouldn't be able to extend our networks." That kind of respect not only enriches the collegial experience; it also fosters cooperation, and ultimately, collaboration.

Louis noted that when respect prevails employees feel emboldened. They know that when someone is disrespectful, others—not living the values of the company—have the authority to challenge them, even if that individual is their boss. Respect fuels the emotional connectedness people feel toward their colleagues and their workplace, and for that reason, they want to act in ways that preserve and strengthen that culture.

By contrast, lack of respect leads to people acting selfishly, hoarding information because they do not trust you. Often that lack of trust is institutional; when organizations work in silos one function does not know another silo and so there is a lack of trust. Cooperation becomes impossible. When you have respect for others, then you can build a sense of mutuality. People want to work with each other because they know they share similar values.

The Best Practice Institute has been studying the issue of respect in the workplace. As Carter told Alisa Cohn of *Forbes.com*, love for the workplace "is the intersection of intense feelings towards aspects of a company, perception of how your company feels about you, and attitudes toward respect and treatment of employees." According to BPI's study, "Most Loved Workplace," when employees feel love for where they work, they want to do a good job because they feel emotionally connected. And when employees feel connected, they want to do right by themselves, their colleagues, and their company.

According to the "Most Loved Workplace "study, respondents who loved their workplace were "between 2 and 4 times more likely to produce more for their organization." Likewise, when employees feel connected to colleagues, 95% say they are more likely to stay with their company. As a result, turnover goes down.

The ways to foster love, or emotional connectedness in the workplace, are straightforward. As Alisa Cohn reported, Carter recommends thanking people for their contributions, celebrating success, using failure as an opportunity to learn, and providing means for employees to connect personal goals to organizational goals. Putting those ideas into practice is rooted in the notion of respect, valuing others because they have something to contribute.[32]

Learning from a Generous Colleague

Belief in ourselves often comes when we are reminded of it by others. Colleagues we remember best are those who teach us the most. My local public radio station, Michigan Radio, broadcast a remembrance of a recently departed colleague, Mark Brush. The remembrance took the form of a conversation between two colleagues, Lester Graham and Rebecca Williams. For Lester, Mark was not a solo actor; he was an individual who was always encouraging others to do their best and helping them do so. For Rebecca, Mark symbolized how to live life with purpose—by looking out for others. Lester and Rebecca noted Mark's professionalism with their colleague and how he was always willing to go the extra mile to get the right information to flesh out a story more fully.

What caught my attention most was their mention of how Mark had connected so well with new staffers. He was not only professional; he was helpful. Mark went out of his way to help others learn how things work in order to do their jobs better. For example, as posted on the website, Jennifer Guerra, news reporter, said, "Mark's the only one I know of who would take his headphones off every time—and I mean every time—someone came up to ask him a question . . . And yet if someone needed his help, he'd stop what he was working on, take his headphones off all the way, turn to the person, and listen. I can't highlight enough how rare that is . . . He was fully present, patient, and generous with his time. Removing his headphones may seem like an insignificant detail, but it speaks volumes." One former employee, Jenn White, summed up Mark with two words: "Kindness and joy . . . He was one of the kind[est] people I've ever known. He was kind with no expectation of applause or recognition. It's just who he was. He was also filled with an irrepressible joy."

The poet Maya Angelou famously said, "I've learned that people will forget what you said, people will forget what you did, but people will never forget how you made them feel." Far be it from me to disagree with Ms. Angelou but—as evidenced by how colleagues remembered Mark—people do remember what you do. What people recalled were his specific actions because those actions were directed not at himself but at others. His actions were focused on the greater good in two ways. Mark wanted to do better journalism, so he pushed himself as he encouraged others. At the same time, he was not so driven that he allowed himself to have cut him off from others. He made himself available to assist others in doing their work.

In doing so, Mark affirmed the real intention of Maya Angelou's quote: he made others feel good about themselves and their work. After his death, Mark Brush earned posthumously the Michigan Association of Public Broadcasters Public Media Impact award. In his nomination letter to the association, Executive Director and General Manager Stephen Schram noted that Mark had won many awards, including a Scripps Howard Award for helping the station to cover the Flint water crisis. Schram also cited Mark's mentoring efforts as well as his creation of the station's first online news internship.

Being a good colleague comes down to being willing to meet people where they are and offer something of yourself. You are serving them because they need you. Those needs may be related to the task at hand or something that is happening outside of the workplace. Colleagues you can count on are colleagues you will remember for the rest of your work life . . . or maybe, your entire life. [33]

RESPECT IS HONORING OTHERS—AS WELL AS YOURSELF—IN A SPIRIT OF HONESTY, INTEGRITY, AND DIGNITY.

Respect: What the Leaders Say

Respect is fundamental to human dignity. How it plays out in our lives is the reflection of grace at work.

***

"Respect starts with the golden rule," says Scott Moorehead. "You first have to start to treat people the way that you want to be treated, to be more refined in your respect. Then ultimately, you have to understand how people want to be treated. You have to combine your inner awareness with empathy for the other person."

For Alaina Love, respect is "appreciating the other individual even if the person may think differently than you. It's demonstrating a degree of intellectual curiosity about their perspectives and their experiences, what may have led them to come to the belief system that they have."

"Respect always has an implication of honoring boundaries,

honoring a person's innate dignity, honoring the right to make decisions, and honoring personal integrity," says Sally Helgeson.

And Mike McKinney states, "Respect has to come from a place of humility that values others simply because they are, simply because they exist. And respect, for me, rests on our shared humanity." He continues by saying, "That's what we have as a common denominator that should generate this kind of respect. It comes from setting aside ego and esteeming others as better than ourselves."

Alan Mulally believes that "One of the most important things as a person and as a leader is awareness in the biggest sense, awareness of yourself, who you are as a person and what you believe, your hopes and dreams." That includes the acknowledgement of others. Knowing oneself as a leader requires him or her to "create an environment where people respect each other and listen to each other and appreciate each other and working together effectively is what's going to make the greatest good for all of us."

Respect "is a mindset. It's how we see people," says Stephen M.R. Covey. "You reverence people. You see the dignity of every person so that we respect everyone as a human being. Because of the dignity of each person."

Stephen quotes his father and namesake, Dr. Stephen Covey, who said, "Leadership is communicating people's worth and potential so clearly that they're inspired to see it in themselves." Stephen says he would add the word "seeing" as in "noticing" to the first part of his Dad's statement. "Seeing it is an act of leadership. It is acting on behalf of another because you communicate it in a way" they realize it for themselves. That is a form of respect.

"I believe that respect is something that we have to practice giving, not just practice earning," says Tim Sanders. "It's like, if you want people to trust you? Trust them first. You want people to respect you? Respect them first."

***

Think about these questions:

- What does it mean to act with respect?

- How does lack of respect affect your life?

- What can you do to practice respect toward others?

- Think about an occasion when you "big-timed" someone, i.e., acted as the other person was "beneath" you. What would you do differently now?

- What does it mean to listen to someone before you offer advice?

- Consider one thing you could do to live more simply?

- How can you make time to reflect on your work?

Graceful Leadership Steps

Respect: *Putting the needs of others before your own*

- Assume good intentions first. Look for the best in others.

- Regard your colleagues as people first—living, breathing women and men who have talents and skills you and your team can use.

- Treat others as "neighbors" in your community of life.

- Practice humility e.g. itemize your limitations as well as your strengths.

- Avoid acting as if you are the "smartest person" in the room.

- Be the leader others want to follow because you back your words with actions and hold yourself accountable for results.

"Do stuff. Be clenched, curious. Not waiting for inspiration's shove or society's kiss on your forehead. Pay attention. It's all about paying attention. Attention is vitality. It connects you with others. It makes you eager. Stay eager."

—Susan Sontag

Action

A is action, *the mechanism for change.*

Change is inherent to the human condition. We are born. We mature. We die. While we cannot control the first step, how we live conditions how we live our lives and in what state we will leave our place in this world. Those with a bias for action will be those who look at life as a gift that rewards us only if we are willing to return that gift through our actions.

Answering the Call to Action

Dr. Mona Hanna-Attisha's introduction to the Flint water crisis did not come from her patients. It came at a gathering of friends from high school, one of whom was Elin Betanzo. She had worked for the Environmental Protection Agency in Washington a decade previously when the agency had dealt with a contaminated water problem. Elin told Mona that untreated water contains lead. As a pediatrician, Dr. Mona knew something else about lead; it was asymptomatic in children. Its presence is only revealed through blood tests.

Dr. Mona was shocked. "It is Michigan, literally, in the middle of the largest source of freshwater in the world. Despite that, there are laws and regulations, and there are people whose main job is to make sure our waters safe," Dr. Mona told Cynthia Canty of Michigan Radio's Stateside program. The problem with Flint's water was the result of cost-savings. The city, then under a state-mandate, had switched from using water from Lake Huron to water from the Flint River. Worse, it was coming through the untreated lead pipes and its corrosive effect leeched the lead from pipes into the drinking supply.

"I am not a patient person, I'm an action person," Dr. Mona says.. A month's worth of research had turned up some alarming data about the danger to the drinking water. "I wanted to get this out as soon as possible because I wanted people to take precautions, so I was relieved. I was ready for that press conference. I wanted to shout these results from a mountaintop." Dr. Mark Watson of Virginia Tech had already discovered contamination. Still, no authorities were listening. "It never should have gotten to the point of me. So, when I think of this crisis, I think of it as a series of dominoes and I am the last domino. It should have stopped when that first mom said, 'Hey there's something wrong with my water.'"

Immediately state authorities, sought to discredit her research. "The state said that I was an unfortunate researcher, that I was causing near-hysteria, that I was splicing and dicing numbers," Hanna-Attisha said on *Fresh Air*. "It's very difficult when you are presenting science and facts and numbers to have the state say that you are wrong." She readily agrees that she and her colleagues broke protocol by announcing results so early but this was a time of crisis where the cost of inaction outweighed action. "I realized that my science, my facts, my evidence, my research was about numbers.

But that every single number in my research was a kid, was a child, was one of my Flint kids," Hanna-Attisha told Michigan Radio's "Stateside" program "And it is those kids and it was their names and it was their faces that woke me up and put me back in this ring and got me to fight back for them."

"The consequences of lead exposure are something we don't readily see." Dr. Mona told Terry Gross on *Fresh Air*. "It impacts, at a population level, cognition, so actually drops the IQ of a population of children, shifting that IQ curve to the left where you have more children who need special education services, less gifted kids." It leads to behavioral problems as well as cognitive ones.

While there is no cure for lead poisoning, Dr. Mona and colleagues did not stand down. "Our response in Flint has been very proactive and preventative, because we cannot ethically wait to see the consequences of lead poisoning, of lead exposure, so we have put into place multiple, multiple interventions that we know that will promote children's brain development and limit the impact of this crisis." Lead poison is not the only toxin kids in poor communities face. "Growing up in poverty is a toxic stress," says Dr. Mona. "Being exposed to violence, lack of nutrition, unsafe places to play—all of these are toxic stresses. And now recently, with the incredible science of brain development, we've learned that all this repetitive stress and trauma for children impacts their entire life course trajectory in a very graded and predictable way."

Born in England Dr. Mona is the child of Iraqi immigrants who settled in Michigan where there was a large population of Iraqi Christians in the greater Detroit area. Her father, however, landed a post-doctoral research position at Michigan Tech, located at the tip of the Keweenaw Peninsula in Michigan's Upper Peninsula (aka the UP), some twelve hours distance by car.

It was an incident that occurred on one of those long journeys back and forth from the UP to the Detroit area to visit family that triggered Mona's interest in medicine. The car in which she was riding in hit black ice and spun out of control. Mona said on "State-side" that upon reaching the hospital, "My mom noticed that my face was crooked." Later young Mona noticed the presence of someone else. "This young doctor was dark-skinned, she had dark hair, she had a white coat on, and she held my hand and said, 'You were in a terrible accident. You are going to be okay,'" she said. Mona was five years old.

The title of her memoir, *What the Eyes Don't See*, takes its name from a professor of pediatrics Mona trained under. He told residents that if they did not study deeply enough, they would not be able to recognize a condition present in a child. Such study breeds awareness and it's that mindset that has fueled Dr. Mona in her quest to protect the youngest and most vulnerable among us. As she writes her book, she tells us, "This is a story of resistance, of activism, of citizen action, of waking up and opening your eyes and making a difference in our community . . . I wrote this book to share the terrible lessons that happened in Flint, but more importantly, I wrote this book to share the incredible work that we did, hand in hand with our community, to make our community care about our children."[34]

Think Big

Organizational leadership requires individual action—as we have seen in the actions of Dr. Mona Hanna-Attisha. And for that reason, I recall a quote from a book jacket blurb. S.C. Gwynne praised author Sebastian Junger for thinking, writing, and doing well in his book, *Tribe: On Homecoming and Belonging*. Specifically, Gwynne said the book demonstrated "the clarity of (Junger's) thought, the elegance of his prose, and the provocativeness of this chosen subject."

Not only do Gwynne's words ring as praise for Junger, they serve as a challenge to leaders: think deeply, communicate clearly, and do something important. The best leaders are those who possess two powerful qualities: self-awareness and humility. The first lets us know our shortcomings; the second keeps us honest about them.

With apologies to Gwynne—himself an author—I will massage his prose into three short declaratives for leaders.

Think deeply. The whirl of today accelerates movement but it does little to facilitate thought. In fact, it may harm it. We are so busy doing we do not think so much about what we do and why we do it. Therefore, it falls to a leader who disciplines self and team to slow down thinking so they breathe deeply. This applies to assessing assumptions as well as looking beyond organizational horizons to discern trends that may affect what happens now and in the future.

Communicate clearly. People are looking for direction. Only someone who understands his or her needs can connect in ways that provide meaning. Good leaders are those that can frame a message in terms that people understand because it echoes their aspirations. Such framing occurs through patient listening and intelligent observation.

Provoke action. Mobilizing others for a common cause is a leader's chief responsibility. Doing it well calls for the ability to connect intention with purpose. When that occurs, people want to get on board and do what they can to help because, as historian James MacGregor Burns writes in his book, *Leadership,* that the values of the leader are echoed in the values of the follower. The leader-follower combination acts in unison to fulfill mutual goals.

Thinking, communicating, and provoking. These three simple words when channeled appropriately can focus a leader's attention on the issues both present and distant, generate ways to address them, and then provoke self and others to take action. It falls to the leader to mobilize others to action around a central purpose.

Acting on a Vision

When considering the desire for action—our purpose—we are wise to ask: from where does purpose come? From a dream or from our vision? And if so, is there a difference between a dream and a vision?

Native Americans, prior to adaptation to Western Civilization, made extensive use of visions. The Sioux tribes of the Plains, which were comprised of multiple bands including the Oglala, Lakota, and Hunkpapa, made extensive use of visions. According to Nathaniel Philbrick's book *The Last Stand: Custer, Sitting Bull, and the Battle of the Little Big Horn*, Sitting Bull, a Hunkpapa chief, put himself through a grueling sun dance. During the hours-long ritual upon in which the flesh is pierced and the body hung backwards, Sitting Bull experienced a vision of the impending invasion of Custer's 7th Calvary.

Sitting Bull predicted that Custer's troops would fall into a kind of funnel and that they would come from a southerly direction. Sitting Bull used this vision to rally the many tribes—perhaps, the largest Native American war party of all time—together to fight Custer. His vision proved true. The 7th Calvary entered from the south and fell into a trap (funnel) laid by Sitting Bull and his three thousand warriors at a grassy hillock nearby a river named the Little Big Horn.

While this vision came to Sitting Bull in a dream, he turned it into an organizational plan as a means of defending his people from an invading army of blue coats. In contemporary business, visions are similarly strategic. You consider where you want to go, where you want to take the organization. Today we have dispensed with the sun dance, but many organizations go through a visioning process. To my way of thinking, vision is "becoming"—you dream of possibility and you seek to put it into action. Note that vision is not mission. Mission is the doing; it is execution. But you cannot execute if you don't know where you are headed. Should we care that we dream, or we vision? *Yes.* Dreams are drifts of the imagination as if one imaginary cloud in the sky. Visions are scripted efforts to effect change. They occur personally and organizationally. For example, a person may dream of becoming a doctor, i.e., what it would be like to help people who are sick. A person who becomes a physician translates that dream into a course of rigorous study and training.

A visionary is one who sees potential in an idea—not always his or her own—and sees its possibilities. Visionaries are ones who power our future. Dreamers are those who may entertain us with their flights of fancy that typically blow away quickly, like puffy clouds on a warm spring day. Nice, but not memorable. Visionaries turn fancy into practice and in this way make the world different for themselves and the rest of us. While visions emerge from our dreams, dreams by themselves are not visions. Dreams are flights of fancy. Visions are *directives*.

Ethical Action

For Dr. Mona Hanna-Attisha, action is a commitment to do better. It is rooted in her principles. Ethical behavior is a proactive process. It is rooted in character; how you behave is a reflection of your moral code. When you surrender your moral character through your actions, you cede your authority to serve as an example to others.

Partisanship abides in darker recesses of our human nature; it's about winning at all costs. Partisans comfort themselves that their side is in the right, and therefore, whatever they do is correct. Abraham Lincoln wrote, "my concern is not whether God is on our side; my greatest concern is to be on God's side, for God is always right. Human values as they relate to morality, equality, and dignity are bedrock principles that when cast aside allow aberrant and abhorrent behaviors to flourish. The least among us become the most-preyed upon. Ethics, therefore, knows no party. Living by a moral code is putting into practice what you believe is right. That is, you call out men who abuse women—as well as all those who give the abusers sanctuary.

Living by a moral code demands that such men be exposed for their predatory behaviors. It also demands protection for their accusers. Justice may be applied retroactively but ethics are lived *proactively*. That is, when we hold ourselves to moral standards, we make it known that behaviors that defile human dignity are not tolerated.

We also do so with the knowledge that not everything changes but that nothing will change unless we ourselves take the first step.[35]

Moral Leadership

People do look for moral clarity and one place they are finding it is where they work. Employees expect higher ethical standards from management. According to a study of 500 employees, conducted by LRN, and published in 2018:

- 83% said following the "Golden Rule" enables companies to make better decisions;

- 62% said managers would do better if they relied upon moral authority; and

- 59% said organizations would be more successful with challenges if their leadership had more moral authority.

Unfortunately, according to the LRN survey called "The State of Moral Leadership Authority in Business," employees are not getting what they expect.

- Only 23% of employees said managers are moral leaders;

- Just 17% stand up for people who were treated unfairly.

- A mere 12% say managers make time to speak to them about why work is meaningful.

- At the same time, 60% of employees say that their direct managers ask for, or expect loyalty from them.

Clearly then, when it comes to moral authority, there is a disconnect between what is expected and what is delivered. So, what can managers do to fulfill their employee's expectations? First, let's cover what not to do—preach! Employees don't want words; they want actions. They also do not expect to have to follow a particular religious creed at work. Just as with the separation of church and state, there is an implied separation in the workplace.

LRN advocates doing two things: firstly, pause to reflect on the situation as a means of connecting with values; and secondly, act with humility. The former may be easier than the latter, but it is only with humility that leaders connect more realistically with others. If you act your title, you set up barriers to understanding. If you act as a leader, you open the door to greater understanding.

Dov Seidman, CEO of LRN, advises leaders to instill purpose, elevate and inspire individuals and live your values. Very importantly in this report, Seidman challenges leaders to embrace moral challenges as he says, by "constant wrestling with the questions of right and wrong, fairness and justice, and with ethical dilemmas." The virtue of this last point is simple: don't take morality for granted. Every organization will say it is publicly doing what's right and ethically avoiding what's wrong. But internally there are men and women of power and influence who either assume all is well or ignore obvious problems. And that's when trouble strikes.

Few people go into business to be transgressors, but transgressions occur because people are people and can make poor choices. Furthermore, avoiding right and wrong is one thing. Deciding between two rights is the tougher choice. Those questions touch on how you do business, what you sell, how you promote and sell as well as how you recruit, retain, and promote employees. A leader who is vigilant on the behavior of others and importantly holds himself to ethical standards is one that can help, as Seidman says, "build moral muscle." Leaders, then as LRN urges, can empower employees to act on their values and build a culture where moral values resonate.[36]

Civility: A Healthy Dose

Over the past decade levels of civility have been declining in America society. The reasons for this are many: fear of the other, resentment at success, as well as political fear mongering. The rise of social media, too, has contributed; people can voice their displeasure, impersonally and often anonymously. Whatever the causes, the effects of incivility are real.

Before exploring further, it is useful to consider the example of our First President. George Washington believed in civility as a matter of course. As a teenager, he handwrote the *Rules of Civility & Decent Behavior in Company and Conversation.* Originally compiled by the Jesuits in 1595, Washington used them as a reference for living an improved life. To the modern reader some of the 110 rules seem odd, if not humorous:

> *9th: Spit not in the Fire, nor Stoop low before it neither Put your Hands into the Flames to warm them, nor Set your Feet upon the Fire especially if there be meat before it.*

> *16th: Do not Puff up the Cheeks, Loll not out the tongue, rub the Hands, or beard, thrust out the lips, or bite them or keep the Lips too open or too Close.*

The majority, however, are as relevant now as they were centuries ago.

> *1st: Every Action done in Company, ought to be with Some Sign of Respect, to those that are Present.*

> *48th: Wherein you reprove Another be unblameable yourself; for example, is more prevalent than Precepts.*

56th: Associate yourself with Men of good Quality if you Esteem your own Reputation; for 'tis better to be alone than in bad Company.

Rules such as these remind us of what it means to behave in public, not simply to be polite, but rather to be respectful of others. The nature of civility is to treat others with the dignity they deserve.[37] Washington himself read deeply. He knew the classics in Greek and Latin and from them, he discerned a code of living which he practiced as a military officer and later as president. Moreover, Washington's ability to remain composed yet present was most evident during the Continental Convention in 1787. Historians note that while he often did not engage in debate, his presence in the room in Philadelphia, while the founding fathers were haggling over the articles of the Constitution, was instrumental toward shaping the atmosphere in the room where people who disagreed could come to agreement for the greater good—the formation of a new nation. For his effort, Washington was selected as President, a job he neither sought nor wanted, but due to his commitment to a higher purpose, he accepted the post.[38] After all the 110th rule of Civility is "Labor to keep alive in your breast that little spark of celestial fire called conscience."

Today it seems as if we have abandoned the example our fore-fathers set. According to the Civility in America 2018, an annual study conducted by Weber Shandwick, there has been a forty percent uptick in "incivility encounters per week" between 2016 and 2018. At the same time, Americans do value the need for civility. Respondents to the survey regarded it as essential to "national pride" and capacity to defuse "tension and conflict." Not surprisingly then, people believe that "restoring civility to our nation" is possible.

While incivility may be on the rise in many sectors, one area where civility reigns is in the workplace. Nine in ten of those surveyed felt civility is prevalent at work. Looking more closely, however, just one-half of those employees felt its leadership was civil.

The situation is worse in workplaces where incivility occurs; less than half of employees trusted management to "handle complaints about incivility." When incivility is not checked, reports of "uncivil comments" rise. As the study shows employees expect leaders to step up to the challenge and "enforce civility in the workplace." Toward this end, just over 40% of Americans surveyed believe there is a need for civility training as well as an "encouragement" from management to report incivility.[39]

Acting Against Incivility

Some cities are trying to do something about this problem. One city is Duluth, Minnesota. In 2003, it launched a program called "Speak Your Peace: The Civility Project." Gerald Seib of the *Wall Street Journal* reported that Speak Your Peace grew out of financial distress. The city was on the verge of bankruptcy and could default on its employees' health insurance. By working together, city and business leaders found a way forward toward civil discussion of these highly charged issues. All levels of local government got involved and developed nine rules for speaking. Conveniently, they all fit on a wallet card.

The rules, according to its website and taken from P.M. Forni's book *Choosing Civility*, focus on respect for others, listening, inclusivity, agreeability, responsibility, and the need to apologize if things go wrong. "The purpose of the Speak Your Peace Civility Project," according to its website, "is to urge the citizens of the Duluth/Superior area to communicate in a more respectful and effective way. This is not a campaign to end disagreements. It is a campaign to improve public discourse by simply reminding ourselves of the very basic principles of respect." Duluth's financial prospects have improved. Mayor Emily Larson to Seib, "Civility is about listening." When people find a common interest, it "lays the groundwork for the next conversation."[40]

Fortunately, political fissures do not prevent people from working together on issues of importance. Columnist Thomas Friedman of the *New York Times* spent some time in Lancaster, Pennsylvania. Locals had formed different kinds of clubs to attack issues of the economy and the vitality of the community; it signified that time was running out and no one was coming to the rescue, so townspeople had to save themselves. Sounds more like a scene from a Western than an Eastern story from Pennsylvania.

Groups solicited information from experts around the country and the world and invited them to come to Lancaster to speak. Partisanship fell by the wayside as citizens saw results of the groups' efforts—a new minor league ballpark, new restaurants, a new hotel and mostly an improved sense of civic pride. Friedman, himself an environmental globalist and early technology adopter, writes, "Not a single community leader I spoke to in Lancaster said the progress was due to technology—to microchips. They all said it was due to relationships—relationships born not of tribal solidarity but of putting aside tribal differences to do big hard things together in their collective interest. It's a beautiful thing to see."

Civil Connections

Relationships are the connections we make that when tightened can create positive change. James and Deborah Fallows found similar stories in their cross-country trek across America. Jim, a one-time speechwriter for Jimmy Carter and long-time journalist and author, is a private pilot. Together he and Deborah visited many towns and what they found inspired a book, *Our Towns: 100,000 Mile Journey into the Heart of America*. Their approach, which Jim wrote about for *The Atlantic* where he has been writing for decades, was to visit a town and have conversations with people. They avoid national issues and rather asked people how their town had changed in the past ten years. Discussions like that led them to discover how townspeople everywhere are sidelining perceived differences in order to work on issues of importance to their local communities.

As Jim explained, "When they arrived in a new place, they would ask, 'Who makes this town go?'" The answers varied widely. Sometimes it was a mayor or a city council member. Sometimes it was a local business titan or real-estate developer. Sometimes a university president or professor, a civic activist, an artist, a saloon-keeper, a historian, or a radio personality . . . What mattered was that the question *had* an answer." It was "a local patriot," heavily invested in helping make a viable future for the place.[41]

People see a problem and rather than wait for a solution they set about making one for themselves. A key to relating to a community is connecting. That is a theme that *New York Times* columnist David Brooks explores in many of his columns. One story he told is that of a woman in Baltimore, Susan Hemminger, who has started a mentoring program for academic underachievers called *Thread*.

It works on the model of a family with volunteers serving as elders who work as coaches to help support the students as they progress through school. One group is known as "Collaborators;" they are specialists who can offer legal, mental health, and even SAT coaching. Holding the system together are paid staffers known as "Community Managers." Gaining the trust of the kids takes time because so many children have been let down by adults in their lives. *Thread* hangs in there with the kids.

"Unconditional love is so rare in life that it is identity-changing when somebody keeps showing up even when you reject them. It is also identity-changing to be the one rejected," says Hemminger. "There is no way to repair national distrust without repairing individual relationships one by one," writes Brooks. "This is where American renewal begins."[42]

Brooks profiles another community action group doing similar work in Spartanburg, South Carolina. Calling itself the Spartanburg Academic Movement (SAM), the group's intention is to help children from low-income backgrounds succeed in school. As is done with "I Promise," the effort is focused on the whole person. The program works long-term tracking the progress of students over decades.

Brook notes that SAM is what some call "collective impact." As Brooks notes the goals are management and therefore encourage people to become involved. Rather than seeking broach changes, the effort is focused on civic involvement. This effort is part of a greater national movement call Strive Together. Their methodology, which began a decade or so ago, focuses on creating a "backbone organization" that as Brooks writes "that can bring all the players together; coordinate decision-making and action; share accountability."

Efforts like SAM are citizen inspired and citizen run. They seek to partner with existing systems (schools and government) when possible, but at the same time, seek to bring in people to help the group achieve its aims. It is relationship building, says Brooks, and from that positive outcomes can result.[43]

Civility in the face of tragedy

Truly civil societies reveal their strength in times of tragedy. When the murder of 11 Jews at the Tree of Life synagogue in Pittsburgh left many speechless, it fell to local leaders to help the nation its bearings.

"These are good, decent people, said Rabbi Jeffrey Myers of those who were slain. Myers was holding service at Tree of Life at the time of the shooting. "They didn't have an ounce of hate in any of them. We turn to the leaders of our country. We've got to stop hate, and it can't just be to say we need to stop hate. We need to do, we need to act, to tone down rhetoric. Hate is not welcome here in Pittsburgh. It should not be welcome in our borders at all.

"We fight hate with love," said Bill Peduto, mayor of Pittsburgh, "We fight it with compassion. We fight it with an understanding that a neighborhood like Squirrel Hill is the most diverse in all of Western Pennsylvania, is a welcoming community that welcomes everyone. It's a community whose foundation is based on that understanding."

Dr. Jeffrey Cohen, president of Allegheny General Hospital where the shooter was taken, said that at least three of those treating him were Jewish. "We're here to take care of sick people" not "judge" them. Cohen, who is also a congregant at Tree of Life, later told reporters that he had spoken to the shooter. "You can't, on one hand, say we should talk to each other, and then I don't talk to him. So, you lead by example, and I'm the leader of the hospital."

Leaders facing crisis would do well to recall these words. Neither called for revenge, nor did they hurl insults and invectives. This is what sensible leaders do. No matter what such leaders may feel inside, they think before they speak. They focus not on themselves, but on the needs of others—on healing. While this sentiment has largely prevailed throughout American history, it sorely lacks today. Leaders who speak with civility and integrity bring us together. Those who speak with grievance and hatred tangle us in their web of deceit and hate.

One president who knew his role in times of tragedy was Ronald Reagan. His remarks after the Challenger disaster are remarkable not simply for their eloquence (penned in part by Peggy Noonan) but also for their human touch. Not only did Reagan seek to comfort the families of the astronauts who died, but he also took an extra step. "I want to add that I wish I could talk to every man and woman who works for NASA or who worked on this mission and tell them: 'Your dedication and professionalism have moved and impressed us for decades. And we know of your anguish. We share it.'" Leaders seek to reach the hearts of everyone in times of tragedy.

Reverend Liddy Barlow, a minister who spoke at a memorial service for the synagogue victims, noted that the "tree of life" phrase appears at the beginning of the Hebrew Bible and at the end of the Christian Bible, citing as the fulfillment of the Garden of Eden. "If that's what the tree looks like, imagine what the neighborhood looks like," Reverend Barlow said. "I think it looks like Squirrel Hill--the city of God."[44]

A few weeks later at an airfield in Dover, Delaware a young widow spoke eloquently of her husband, Major Brent Taylor, who had been killed in Afghanistan. Her words, so purposeful and heartfelt, reminded us that maintaining civility can sometimes exact a price.

Brent Taylor also served as mayor of North Ogden, Utah and was the kind of person, interim mayor Brent Chugg told NPR's Rachel Martin, who "made you feel good to be around." Taylor was 39 and left behind a wife and seven children ranging from 11 months to 13 years old.

Utah Governor Gary Herbert knew Taylor personally and said he had advised him not to do a fourth tour. "You've done enough. You've done your part." Taylor insisted, however, says Governor Herbert. "He thought he could do some good, to help people be liberated. That's an admirable quality that we call ought to emulate."

That kind of service was evident in his leadership. "He was an outstanding mayor," says Chugg. "He was very progressive. He moved this city forward in a very positive way." Taylor was not a partisan. "He wasn't a politician he was a statesman. He was kind to everyone. You felt good in his presence. He always had a smile on his face. He remembered your name. He was very personable."

That style endeared Taylor to the citizens of North Ogden who re-elected him as mayor as well as to city employees to whom he "showed love and respect." Chugg adds, "I will miss his friendship. He was a truly a great friend someone you loved and respected and could trust. Made you feel welcome where ever you were."

Whether he was at home in North Ogden or with the people of Afghanistan, Taylor's calling was the service to others. In his remembrance of Taylor, Governor Herbert posed the question that anyone in leadership should ask: "What can we do to help our fellow man?"

After her husband's funeral, Jenny Taylor spoke to CNN from the city offices of North Ogden, Utah where her husband had served as mayor. Again, she was resolute and steadfast. She told CNN that there were up days and down and that she and her seven children were holding their own. Since Brent was not expected home until January or February it still felt as if his absence was planned and that one day soon he would come home. She closed her interview showing the flag that had draped her husband's casket and the medals he had been awarded posthumously. She admitted receiving the Purple Heart had been hard because she knew the sacrifice it took to earn it.

In an era when public service may not be as respected as it once was, Brent Taylor reminds us that working for a cause greater than yourself – be it in uniform or in your community – comes down to working to make things better for people. And Taylor did it gladly with an open heart, a kind word, and ready smile. Service to the community as an elected official is not about winning nor losing elections. It is about making things better for citizens individually and collectively. It requires participation.[45]

Organizational Responsibility

Well-run organizations have a degree of institutional pride that stems from their spirit of civility. It may be expressed in words on wall posters or wallet cards, but it reinforced by the example its managers, especially those at the top, set. When employees see that management lives its example, they understand that doing what's right is not a saying; it's a practice. So how does it manifest itself outside of customer service? Well, to my way of thinking, service is service. While we may not have an external customer, we likely have people in our lives with whom we have regular contact. Striving to do what's right behaviorally toward that stakeholder requires a combination of ethics, civility, and comity. Let's take them one at a time.

Ethics. It should never go without saying that honesty and integrity matter. Management must make it a point of pride for employees to make the right call when it comes to making ethical choices. Managers who flout compliance on small things, say expense reports, send the message that it's okay to cheat as long as you don't get caught.

Civility. Organizations, where employees treat others with respect, are those where behavioral norms are evident. Very often such organizations have values propositions that hold employees accountable for speaking respectfully, doing right by colleagues, and treating customers and stakeholders as intelligent people worthy of good service.

Comity. People get along with one another. Not because they are saints but because there is an expectation of respecting the work and respecting the dignity of those who do it. Comity is a sense of peacefulness. It does not mask conflict; it supersedes it. That is, people can disagree (and in fact should disagree at times) over issues, but they do not need to make those disagreements personal. Comity ensures that people keep the peace.

Ethics, civility, and comity are virtues that organizations must work to instill and put into practice. At the same time, we human beings will make mistakes. We will behave in ways that hurt people, we will disrespect one another, and we will be disagreeable. When these problems occur, management must intervene and discipline the transgressors. Failure to do so erodes the value systems. Providing means for transgressors to make amends validates the values and provides those who make mistakes a chance to right their wrongs. Organizations whose cultures place a premium on doing what's right are organizations for which employees want to work and customers want to patronize.[46]

Deciding to Decide

What happens when organizations do not abide by the rules of civility? What then should we do? Not long ago I had a conversation with a colleague working in a professional services consulting firm.

My colleague was describing how the head of the firm's behavior was alienating his colleagues, who were—like him—equal partners. Yet the head man insisted on making all decisions himself, ignoring input from others. He tolerated no discussion of problems, refusing to hear any complaints. Worse, he viewed all such problems as challenges to his authority and since he was adept at holding command and utilized control tactics, he swatted all problems with the only tool in his tool kit—a hammer. When my colleague asked for suggestions, I gave him the advice I have given many executives in similar situations, be it a small firm or a large corporation. You have three choices: tolerate, leave, or act. Let's take each one at a time.

Tolerate. Not every problem requires your personal involvement. You only become involved when the situation demands intervention from you. To do otherwise would be what we call meddling. On the other hand, if you do not want to become involved, or feel you cannot do so for reasons of job security, you can ignore the problem by keeping your head down.

Leave. Intolerable situations demand irrevocable decisions. If the problem is so great—and truly beyond your control—you may have to exit the situation. Ignoring it may cause too much pain. There is no shame in leaving an organization that you cannot change and as a result, is making you unhappy.

Act. This is the choice for leaders. Seldom if ever can a leader say, not my problem. She must confront the problem and deal with it realistically. She must find ways to mobilize others to take action to find solutions. Leadership requires active intervention.

One who has met the call to action with courage —and with the physical grace of an athlete—is two-time Olympic gymnast Aly Raisman. She won three medals and helped the USA win the gold at the 2012 Olympics in London. Aly also has a good sense of humor. "It's funny because [my coach] will say I'm the most uncoordinated Olympian in the whole world."

But sadly, there was another side to her story. Aly was one of many hundreds of victims of Dr. Larry Nassar who sexually abused girl and women gymnasts. As she told Dr. Jonathan Lapook on CBS 60 Minutes, Nassar "would always bring me, you know, desserts or gifts. He would buy me little things. So, I really thought he was a nice person. I really thought he was looking out for me. That's why I want to do this interview. That's why I wanna talk about it. I want people to know just because someone is nice to you and just because everyone is saying they're the best person, it does not make it okay for them to ever make you uncomfortable. Ever."

Speaking out takes courage. Speaking out when a trusted adult has abused you, and as all victims of abuse feel, you feel less than worthy, less than credible, takes an immense amount of courage. "I think it's important for people to know too I'm still trying to put the pieces together today. You know it impacts you for the rest of your life." In January 2018, Aly—along with more than 150 young women—testified at Larry Nassar's trial. Justice was served for Nassar who will spend the rest of his life in jail. Justice for the young women he abused will not be assuaged by the monetary settlements. Healing will only come from within as well as with the support and example they receive from fellow survivors like Aly Raisman, who showed grace under courage.[47]

The bottom line is that none of us can control events. We may be able to influence outcomes, but we are not in command. What we can control is how we react to such events. The question arises: what will you do and why? Each of us must answer for ourselves. Stand and fight. Or retreat to fight another day. Or some may choose to just walk away. Each response may be valid. Only the individual can make the call. "If a problem is fixable, if a situation is such that you can do something about it, then there is no need to worry," said the Dalai Lama XIV. "If it's not fixable, then there is no help in worrying. There is no benefit in worrying whatsoever."

Knowing the situation and what you can do about it puts the individual into a position where he or she controls his or her destiny.

And that's a sense of control, the same you might get if you worked to get your body in shape to climb a mountain. The mountain is steep, but you can prepare yourself for the challenge.

Be Prepared to Act

Action requires preparation. And for leaders, part of preparation comes from being ready for the unexpected. There's a question that every leader must ask: when crisis strikes will you be ready? That is a question that every senior leader asks himself, or herself regularly. We like to think that we can be primed and waiting when disaster or tragedy strikes but will we?

One such person who reflected on what it was like to face tragedy not once but twice was C.J. Price, a hospital administrator at Parkland Memorial Hospital. On November 27, 1963, he put down his thoughts in a memo about what it was like to have the eyes of the world on his hospital. Parkland was where President John F. Kennedy and Governor John Connally received emergency treatment for gunshot wounds. Three days later Lee Harvey Oswald, Kennedy's shooter, also received treatment for gunshot wounds. Of these three, only Connally survived.

Parkland, in Price's words, "became the site of the ascendancy of the 36th President" and a de facto "center of the attention of the world." Lyndon Johnson was at Parkland when Kennedy died and so became his successor. [Johnson later was sworn in as President on the tarmac of Dallas airport.] Through it all, Price notes, Parkland "continued to function as close to a normal pace as a large charity hospital."

Price in his memo wonders how Parkland was able to perform. Was it "Spirit? Dedication? Preparedness?" Price concludes that these factors were important, but the differentiating component lay in the people. "People whose education and training is sound. People whose judgment is calm and perceptive. People whose actions are deliberate and definitive." As a result, Price concludes, "Our pride is not that we're swept up by the whirlwind of tragic history, but that when we were, we were not found wanting." The physicians, nurses and staff at Parkland did their part. They answered the call, and while all would have wished for a better outcome for their president, they did answer the call of duty. The hospital continued to meet its obligations.

While the memo is an interesting footnote to a tragic day in history, Price's reflections are invaluable for anyone in leadership seeking to think through a crisis. Preparation, certainly, is important, but you need to have smart, savvy, and resourceful people available. Identifying people who will respond well in a crisis may be akin to playing darts blindfolded. You don't know what you will get. That said, if you hire an individual who is studious, not rash, practiced, not sloppy, and most of all composed and not wild-eyed, you may have the makings of one who can operate under pressure without losing his cool.

Such a person is one whose first instinct may be to take over but knows that doing so undermines the efforts of others. This type leader pushes others to forefront, and only steps up when there is no one else to act. Crises can occur at any time; not necessarily when we expect them. But you can prepare to have the right people with the right plan in place in case of an emergency. [48]

Acting Positively

Sometimes an "emergency" will strike your career. And it may come in a phone call that goes like this: "'Well, Jim, we've decided to go in a different direction.'" That is how Jim Brandstatter, who was the color analyst for 31 years of Detroit Lions broadcasts, learned he had been fired by WJR, the station that broadcasts team's games. Brandstatter admitted he was "hurt" by the decision, for the reason that it came out of the blue. He had called into WJR to tell them that his current contract— which still had three years to run—was fine and good and he was asking for no changes.

What Brandstatter did next is typical Brandstatter. He called back the station and apologized to the executive who had fired him for being short with him. "You took me by surprise." No recriminations, no yelling, no temper tantrums. And then he tweeted the news to his fans who are as loyal to him as the Lions were disloyal to him.

There was one upside. As Brandstatter told the *Detroit News*, "What worries you is you wonder, 'Are you losing your game?' I didn't think I was. I felt I was pretty good. I was on top of stuff. I didn't feel I was losing anything in regard to the professional side, the nuts and bolts, the X's and O's as a color analyst. I don't think that was the case. That's comforting to know from my perspective, that is, that it's not me; it's them."

Carlos Monarrez, a columnist for the Detroit Free Press, marveled at Brandstatter's equanimity. "I couldn't believe how professional he was. The guy had just been canned and he could have unloaded, even just a little . . . But come on. You've just been fired, Brandy. Unleash your animus! Nope. Nothing. There's no animus in Brandstatter. He is who he is: A big teddy bear. Clearly, he was disappointed. But mostly, he was philosophical about his situation."

As Brandstatter told Monarrez, "It probably exceeded in terms of expectations, in regard to your average lifespan of your radio color analyst. So, from that perspective, I feel OK. I would have obviously liked to have gone out on my terms. But you learn in broadcasting that that's probably not the case most often." By way of explanation, Brandstatter was told that the station wanted something new, which is fine but sort of ridiculous in the world of local team sports radio broadcasting. The entire experience is an anachronism. When fans can get local and national television coverage, why listen to the radio? They do it because they like the announcers, imaging them as friends along on the journey we call *the season*.

Fans develop relationships with the broadcasters, who unlike national broadcasters, experience the highs and lows of the team. And with the Lions for the decades it has been chiefly lows. Brandstatter was the loyal fan, the one who while calling out the team and its players for mistakes, always did so from the perspective of loyalty.

He was on our side and we loved him for it. What Brandstatter exemplifies is how to respond gracefully to a bad call. He did not trash the team, nor the station. He went so far as to call himself on the carpet for being abrupt.

Brandstatter solidified his graceful exit by reaching out to his successor in the booth, former Lions All-Pro offensive lineman Lomas Brown. For his part, Brown was grateful, tweeting that he respected Brandstatter and thanked him for the "advice and encouragement" he had offered. In an era with so many celebrities who use their popularity like a shield of entitlement, Brandstatter remains a regular guy. One who knows how to deal with a bad break. With class. [49]

Defining His Character

How an individual handles defeat is a testament to character. Few men have wanted to be president more—and none have come as close—without winning, as John McCain did in 2008. But when you observe how McCain praised his rival, the soon to be president, you realize the character of this man. Witness what McCain said during his concession speech:

"I urge all Americans who supported me to join me in not just congratulating him, but offering our next president our good-will and earnest effort to find ways to come together, to find the necessary compromises, to bridge our differences and help restore our prosperity, defend our security in a dangerous world, and leave our children and grandchildren a stronger, better country than we inherited."

McCain celebrated the election of the nation's first African-American president as a moment of history. Note how McCain makes the victory of his rival as both a national moment as well as a personal one.

"Senator Obama has achieved a great thing for himself and for his country. I applaud him for it and offer my sincere sympathy that his beloved grandmother did not live to see this day—though our faith assures us she is at rest in the presence of her Creator and so very proud of the good man she helped raise."

McCain was never maudlin. When asked if he regretted losing the Republican nomination in 2000, he says "everyday" with a smile. When asked about losing to Obama he cracked, "I sleep like a baby. I wake up every two hours and cry." Having survived five-and-half years in a North Vietnamese prison losing an election was nothing he could not handle. And he did handle the loss with grace, returning to the Senate to continue to fight for the issues he held deal, both internationally and domestically.

Character often shows itself more in adversity than in defeat. Those who wallow in defeat by lashing out at their opponents reveal themselves as weak and insecure. Those, like John McCain, who look at defeat as one misstep in a long journey of making the right steps are those who have the courage of their convictions. They are men and women worthy of following.

Such character comes from introspection. McCain did not spare himself criticism. In the HBO documentary, *John McCain: For Whom the Bell Tolls*, he discusses two incidents where he compromised his own values. The first was when he was accused of receiving special favors from Charles Keating, former head of a failed savings and loan and a convicted felon. While the Senate cleared McCain of wrongdoing, he felt he had let his standards and his constituents down.

Again in 2000, he ducked the controversy over the Confederate flag flying over the capitol building in Charleston, South Carolina. Knowing the issue would be divisive and could cost him votes in the primary McCain remained somewhat neutral on the issue. He lost the primary regardless to George W. Bush. He later lamented he had not been more honest in his criticism of the flag flying on state property.

To McCain integrity was everything. McCain was the son and grandson of four-star admirals. The North Vietnamese knew of McCain's father and offered him an early release from captivity. McCain refused; it was not only against Navy tradition of "last man in, last man out," it would bring harm to the remaining POWs. "I knew that every prisoner the Vietnamese tried to break, those who had arrived before me and those who would come after me, would be taunted with the story of how an admiral's son had gone home early, a lucky beneficiary of America's class-conscious society," McCain wrote in his memoir, *Faith of My Fathers*. Any privilege McCain would receive "would add to the suffering of men who were already straining to keep faith with their country." McCain lived by a code of service that put others first.

McCain revealed his honor further when he defended Barack Obama at a town hall event in Minnesota in the midst of the 2008 campaign. After a woman expressed her fear of Obama, McCain assured her that she had nothing to be afraid of. That comment drew boos from the crowd. Another woman then stood up said she couldn't trust Obama because he was an "Arab." McCain gently took the microphone from her, and shook his head, saying, "He's a decent family man, and citizen, that I just happen to have disagreements with on fundamental issues, and that's what this campaign is all about." Those comments in defense of his opponent may have cost McCain votes, but he certainly lived up to his honor code.

McCain was a mentor to junior senators of both parties. He took them under his wing, as Susan Collins of Maine recalled on CNN. He took her on his trips around the world, including to Iraq. Once on a scary landing, he patted her hand saying that he had been in five air crashes, including the time he was shot down over North Vietnam, and he was certain he would die in his own bed. Humor was important to McCain; it provided levity to the challenges in his life. "In the words of Chairman Mao," McCain liked to joke, "it's always darkest before it's totally black."

Reporters loved McCain because while he would rail against what they had reported upon occasion, or more often, snap at them in private. At the same time, he would call and apologize, if he felt he had been out of line. He had nicknames for reporters as a kind of endearment. While he teased the press, as he did everyone, he believed in a free press as a matter of national security. He told NBC's Chuck Todd, tongue in cheek, "I hate the press. I hate you especially." McCain then turned serious,. "But the fact is, we need you. We need a free press. If you want to preserve democracy ʸ as we know it, you need to have a free· and many times· an adversarial press. And without it, I am afraid that we would lose so much of our individual liberties."

Former Senator Russ Feingold remembered McCain fondly in an op-ed piece for the *New York Times.* The two of them worked across the aisle on many issues, notably the McCain-Feingold campaign reform bill. When the two were in Arkansas speaking, McCain would introduce Feingold by saying that voters in Wisconsin thought their senator's first name was "McCain." The two of them from opposite parties worked across the aisle when possible. On a memorable trip to Baghdad after a briefing on combat operations, Feingold raised some divergent thoughts. A Republican governor who had made the trip asked McCain why he had brought Feingold along, as if everyone on the trip had to toe the line. McCain replied, "I bring Russ along because he is consistent—consistently wrong." Feingold added, "The fact is, as passionate as John was about his positions, he truly valued hearing all sides and was a good listener." He even told Feingold that if he won the presidency, he would make him a cabinet officer, adding as he smiled, "But just not as secretary of defense." As passionate as McCain was, he enjoyed life to the fullest. Feingold notes a time that McCain stayed up into wee hours of the morning playing blackjack at the casino. As serious as he was about issues, he was a good friend and one who loved to have a good time.

Near the end of his 2008 presidential campaign concession

speech, McCain underscored what service meant to him. "I would not be an American worthy of the name, should I regret a fate that has allowed me the extraordinary privilege of serving this country for a half a century. Today, I was a candidate for the highest office in the country I love so much. And tonight, I remain her servant. That is blessing enough for anyone . . ."[50]

Inspiration: Open Your Ears

Recalling the life of men like John McCain—as well as the example of women like Dr. Mona Hanna-Attisha—gives us hope for a better tomorrow. These figures are inspiring. Yet inspiration need not come exclusively from those we regard as heroes, it emerges from people we meet every day, if only we listen.

Such was the case with me one day while riding to the airport to catch a morning flight. Since I was feeling a bit under the weather, I was not in a mood to chat. My disinclination, however, did not stop my driver, whom I will call Jim, from speaking. He casually noted that he was a retired delivery driver with 30 years under his belt. Moments later he was regaling me with a story of a woman he had saved from drowning. It had been a cold winter's day and the woman's car had slipped off the road and skidded into a man-made pond. Jim, after being flagged down by a motorist, stopped his truck, and slid himself down the snowy bank to the water's edge.

Although the temperature was 16 degrees, the pond had not yet frozen and so the woman's car was slipping slowly under. Jim assumed the water was no more than 3 feet deep. It was actually four times this depth. When he found the water over his head, he swam to the car. The window had been rolled down and so Jim tried to pry open the car door. The water pressure prevented such a maneuver. And try as he might, Jim tried to release the woman from the car. She was glassy-eyed and unresponsive. Fearing for his own safety, Jim gave up and headed back for shore.

Heaving himself on the bank he felt horrible, praying aloud for a miracle. The car dipped under the water and seconds later those on shore pointed out that the woman had freed herself from the car. The cold water had shocked her awake and she was calling out that she could not swim. Jim dove into the water headfirst and swam to retrieve her. Jim reached her gloved hand and tugged her toward himself. Jim then towed her and himself to shore.

Reaching the snowy bank, he collapsed. People around the pond brought blankets and covered the woman. An ambulance was en route. Fortunately for Jim, people from the nearby area knew him as their local delivery driver and were willing to assist him, too. Jim pulled himself together enough to get back in his truck and drive to the community clubhouse. There he was stripped and plunged into a hot tub and given hot chocolate. He was a local hero and within an hour the local media, television, radio, and press had descended on the clubhouse. He spent four hours telling his story. He was the breaking news story of Detroit for that day and the next.

While Jim's lifesaving effort made headlines, his commitment to helping others is his daily sustenance. He became active in his church as a counselor. Jim's story is a reminder that we live in a world surrounded by people who make it their mission to share their time with others. I told Jim that he would die a rich man for all the good he has done for others. He is what management thinker and author Adam Grant would call a "giver," a person who finds meaning in helping others. Such people seek no credit for the work they do; they find joy in knowing that they are helping others find a path forward.

President John F. Kennedy, himself a war hero who put himself at risk during the rescue of his sunken PT boat in shark-infested waters, said "A man does what he must—in spite of personal consequences, in spite of obstacles and dangers and pressures—and that is the basis of all morality." So too, it is with service to others. Jim's story reminds us that heroic actions save lives but commitment to serving others lasts for a lifetime. Jim is that rare individual whom many would call heroic for risking his life but many more would call him inspiring for his commitment toward serving others. Such is the nature of inspiration. You can find it anywhere if you simply listen.

ACTING ON BEHALF OF ANOTHER IS ACTING WITH THE INTENTION OF DOING SOMETHING FOR THE GREATER GOOD.

Action: What the Leaders Say

Grace is given without preconditions and so it falls to those who receive it to put it to good use.

***

Action "means to use one's power or influence to help others," says Christine Porath. "Lift others up in some way through smaller, big acts, but ideally to go out of your way to see that someone is taken care of or is included." Exclusion is inherent in our society so for Christine looking to include those on the margins, those outside the mainstream, or even outside the workstream, requires an action on our part.

Part of acting is learning how to give advice in the spirit of helping rather than dictating. Have a conversation. Listen to what someone needs, advises Wayne Baker. Offer your interpretation of what you heard and wait for a response or clarification. "And then I think that you also have to ask for permission to help if it hasn't been requested. You know, that just instead of offering up I could say, "Look, I have some ideas, would you like to hear them?"

Acting with grace requires a sense of respect for others. Tim Sanders poses a hypothetical situation. "If you and I worked together, and you came to me and complained to me about this jerk in the service department, and I went straight to the big boss—because the big boss loves me—and since I'm the top salesperson, I got the jerk in trouble, then I've acted on behalf of my co-worker, but not necessarily with grace."

Alan Mulally, as a former CEO of two major corporations, knows all about acting with the right intentions. "It's about the people, talented people, working together," says Alan. "The job for leaders is to provide that clarity [of purpose] for everybody and to have a plan that delivers profitable growth and clarifies every element of it. Overcommunicate the clarity. Reinforce the clarity with all of our management and human resources' practices and love them up. Love them up." And such an approach is self-reinforcing. According to Alan, "once you agree to the principles, practices, and the management system, you agree to working together. You're making a commitment to each other and yourself that you're going to operate this way."

***

Think about these questions:

- What must you do before you act?

- Why is action essential to effective leadership?

- How will you discipline yourself to distinguish between impulse (*sudden urge*) and action (*thoughtful intention*)?

- What is one action you can take to do something positive for a colleague?

- What does it mean to you to be a "moral leader"?

- How can you demonstrate civility in your life?

- As a leader, what are you doing to prepare for the future?

- How can you act with civility to someone who has treated you disrespectfully?

Graceful Leadership Steps

Action: *Acting for the benefit of others*

- Look for ways to act with intention, that is, putting your best self forward.

- When you make a mistake, apologize, and make amends. (Remember words are cheap; actions make a difference.)

- Make time to deliberate options before making a major decision.

- Take time to dream, e.g. free-associate ideas without making judgments.

- Consider your purpose. How does it complement your vision for what you want to accomplish?

- Practice ways to be a servant leader, e.g. challenge yourself to inspire rather than criticize.

- Find ways to volunteer your services to your community. Itemize your interests and skills and find a match for what you do to those who can benefit: schools, youth teams, community groups, schools, and churches.

Chapter 5

> *"Compassion is the basis of morality."*
>
> — Authur Schopenhauer

Compassion

C **is compassion,** *the concern for others.*

The word "compassion" essentially means "with passion." But passion alone is not enough; it must be conjoined with a sense of others, a community so to speak. That connection comes from the understanding of others as living breathing human beings—as flawed and vulnerable as ourselves—but also as—wondrous and wonderful as human beings can be.

What It Means to Serve Others

You only die once but you live every day. So says John Feal, who lives those words every day in his quest to make life better for others. You see John is a 9/11 responder whose left foot was crushed by an 8,000-steel beam. John was one of the many—in the fact the majority—of non-uniformed first responders who worked at Ground Zero. He spent 11 weeks in hospital eventually losing part of his foot. He also has suffered damage to his spine and knees as a result of his injury. He lives in constant pain.

All of which John uses to motivate himself to go to work every day and help his fellow responders. Feal was one of the individuals who lobbied Congress to get health care for first responders. It took years of "guerilla lobbying"—one elected official at a time—to get action. The James Zagroda Health and Safety Act was passed in 2010 but it took another round of action in 2015 to get it renewed.

In his interview with Terry Gross on NPR's *Fresh Air*, Feal describes himself as an introvert but views what happened to him as a blessing. It was something that profoundly changed him and transformed him into an activist. "I started going to their hearings. And then, the next thing you know, I started taking other Sept. 11 responders to somebody else's hearings, and then the judges and the lawyers were like, 'Oh here comes Feal, with his crew!'" No apologies. As Feal puts it, "The only time I really ever come out of character—if somebody has the ability to help somebody and doesn't do it for a reason that doesn't measure up to my standards, that's when I tend to come out of character. I just don't understand how human beings can be so cold and callous and hurt each other."

Feal founded the Feal Good Foundation to help fellow first responders. The foundation provides for basic needs as well as medical ones. He also makes personal gestures like buying people coffee if he's in line with them. And for good measure, he donated a kidney. John Feal lives the life of service. When you hear about men like Feal, it is both inspiring as well as humbling, even intimidating. How could I do something like that? Reality dictates that you won't and don't have to. You chose what you want to do with your life. Men like John Feal show us that service to others is rewarding. Feal does not view himself as a victim; he's a healer.

Prior to his injury, Feal fancied himself a tough guy—a John Wayne type—ex-Army, physically fit, and a one-time wrestling coach. Now his toughness comes from living with pain but using it as motivation to help others. The lesson that men like Feal teach us that we have something to give. For some, it's a donation to a good cause. For others, it's a gift of self. Your time! Whatever you can do to make a positive difference matters. It's a matter of love. "The measure of love," wrote Bishop Fulton Sheen, "is not the pleasure it gives—that is the way the world judges it—but the joy and peace it can purchase for others." In short, giving is not getting; giving is sharing what you have with others. Simple really, if only we make the time.[51]

Delivering Compassion

Do I belong here? That's a question that John Feal answered for himself. He saw a need to serve and he put himself forward. For others, the calling may be less clear. The reason for their connection to work and the workplace is due to a sense of belonging. Dr. Abraham Maslow, a pioneering social psychologist, ranks "belonging" as third in his Hierarchy of Needs for human satisfaction and fulfillment. Individuals want to feel that they fit in. On one level, they fit because the work is interesting. On another level, they feel connected to their co-workers. And ultimately and ideally, they feel part of the workplace because their work has meaning.

Peter Drucker, the founding thinker of modern management, wrote that executives should treat knowledge workers (a term he coined) as one would treat a volunteer. Drucker, who had a knack for cutting to the heart of the matter, understood that employees who use their brains for one employer could just as easily put those brains to work for another employer. And if a company wanted to retain them, it needed to make them feel welcome.

Organizations that depend upon volunteer labor understand this dynamic intuitively. They know that if someone who does not feel that they fit in, or worse that they are not making a contribution, will go someplace else. In a hurry! Volunteerism springs from a commitment to do good, to make that positive difference. They volunteer because they find satisfaction in helping others. Volunteers who remain with an organization find fulfillment. The same applies to employees who work for hire. Both groups are engaged in what they do and why they do it. In short, they feel a sense of belonging. Belonging is essential to developing that sense of engagement. And here are three ways to nurture it.

Find Purpose. Work without purpose is work; work with purpose can be joy. When people know that what they do matters to others, and how it is connected to what the organization does, then that gives meaning to labor. Purposeful work is work that encourages commitment.

Recognize Results. Work is hard. Life is short. These are two well-worn clichés that can be mitigated when management takes the time to recognize a job well done. Publicize the accomplishments of teams and make note of the people who outperformed the norm. Results should resonate so that everyone knows what has been achieved.

Encourage Camaraderie. Work is not a place to socialize. It is a place to pull together to do the job. That said, when people are united in purpose, they may find affinity with one another. Managers can encourage that connection by creating opportunities for employees to connect in their off-hours through activities that run the gamut from recreational sports, company picnics, or group volunteer events. (One caveat. When it comes to socialization, participation is strictly voluntarily. Forcing people to do something outside of work defeats the essence of belonging.)

There is something else about belonging that was pointed out to me by an executive with whom I was working. He noted that belonging connotes ownership. You belong therefore you own. Not property but something more meaningful. You own responsibility. You have a sense of autonomy that enables you to act for the good of the organization. Not because you have to, but because you want to. Fostering the sense of belonging may be one of a leader's most powerful levers. Used properly it elevates the nature of work with a sense of purpose that brings people together for common cause and encourages them to bond with one another in the work they do.[52]

G-Man for All

Understanding God is Father Gregory Boyle's mission. He practices that faith through the founding and running of his ministry—Homeboy Industries—the world's largest gang intervention and rehabilitation service that he founded in 1988. That is his purpose and where he feels he belongs.

Father Boyle (whom we met briefly in Chapter 3) says he finds God in the example of the thousands of men and women (aka homies) who have been transformed through the simple act of finding a job. It has given them an alternative to gang affiliation and affirms their sense of worth, a sense that most never had because the circumstances of their upbringing were so cruel and depraved.

Homeboy Industries was founded more than 30 years ago as a means of providing employment to gang members in East LA. Few businesses would hire ex-gang members so Father Greg, Jesuit pastor of the Dolores Mission, the poorest mission in the L.A. archdiocese, created a business to provide those jobs. Today Homeboy serves not just the neighborhood, but all of Los Angeles County with its restaurants, coffee shops, bakeries, and even a tattoo removal clinic. Its tattoo removal clinic came about because ex-gang members wanted to remove tattoos no longer relevant to their current lives, and which in some instances, may prevent them from getting hired. Removing a tattoo is a long and painful process but it can serve as a kind of rebirth. Not everything Homebody has tried has been successful, for example, the plumbing business. It seemed terrific as a business proposition, but as Fr. Boyle says wryly, "I guess people didn't feel comfortable having ex-gang members in their houses."

To watch Father Boyle, as I did in a presentation he gave, get choked up telling stories of homies redeemed—stories he has told hundreds of times and written about in his books—is to see a man who knows the Face of God as some would say, because he sees it in the person standing in front of him. Father Boyle's presentation echoes the themes of his second book, *Barking to the Choir: The Power of Radical Kinship*. In the book, he writes about working at the margins of society, finding a problem, and figuring out what might be done. Father Boyle invites people to find the need and see if there is something Homeboy might do.

To outsiders the work may seem grim. To Father Boyle there is joy, even laughter. He tells a story about one of the homies in his ministry who said, "Lord is Exhausted" in a Psalm he was reading. The word was supposed to be "exalted," but Father Gregory liked the homie's version better. He also noted that one of his spiritual directors said we needed a "better" God. You see, in Father Gregory's world many may see God but each of us may perceive Him differently. Hence the God is "exhausted" and may indeed desire a make-over—or at least a better version of how we *perceive* him.

And that's the point. A need arises, and you avail yourself of the opportunity. At the end of near the end of *Barking to the Choir,* Father Boyle writes about "exquisite mutuality."—It is a sense of gratefulness that comes from sharing experience and history with others, where "reciprocal expectations disappear," you do what you do as you share life together.

"I don't empower anyone at Homeboy Industries," writes Father Boyle. "But if one can love boundlessly, then folks on the margins become utterly convinced of their own goodness. We find our awakened connection to each other—a focused, balanced attention to the person in front of us." It becomes, as Fr. Boyle concludes, "An exquisite mutuality, lighting the whole sky."[53]

Mercy, Mercy

Integral to the concept of compassion is mercy. Like grace, mercy is not earned; it is given with the expectation of doing good. While we show mercy toward our transgressors, we also show it toward those in need. When we help another person in need, we are showing mercy that is inherent in grace. There is no expectation of payback; there is only a desire to assist. Grace enables us to take the higher road, to think more clearly.

Mercy is a theme that runs through many of Shakespeare's plays. The heroes of Shakespeare's works exhibit it; the tyrants do not. In *The Merchant of Venice*, Portia, disguised as the lawyer Baltazar, argues in court on behalf of her lover, Antonio. She begs Shylock, to whom Antonio is in debt, for mercy with this soliloquy:

> *The quality of mercy is not strained.*
> *It droppeth as the gentle rain from heaven*
> *Upon the place beneath. It is twice blest:*
> *It blesseth him that gives and him that takes.*

The notion of "twice blessed" gets to the heart of mercy—it's good for giver and receiver both. Portia next elevates mercy to the highest strata of virtues.

> *'Tis mightiest in the mightiest; it becomes*
> *The thronèd monarch better than his crown.*
> *His scepter shows the force of temporal power,*
> *The attribute to awe and majesty*
> *Wherein doth sit the dread and fear of kings;*
> *But mercy is above this sceptered sway.*
> *It is enthronèd in the hearts of kings;*
> *It is an attribute to God Himself;*

Portia argues that mercy, which is from heaven, is "above temporal power." Even better, "It is enthroned in the hearts" of kings. And when put into practice by someone with power, it becomes "an attribute to God Himself."[54]

Winston Churchill was one who sought value in mercy, as reflected in his mantra: "In War: Resolution, In Defeat: Defiance, In Victory: Magnanimity. In Peace: Good Will." Churchill, as this statement indicates, did not shirk the good fight, but when it was over, he believed in grace. He exerted this in his political dealings—although ostracized often from members of his own party, he seldom sought revenge. At the end of World War II, he was for extending the olive branch to Germany to rebuild the shattered nation. That said—Churchill fully supported the Nuremberg Trials that put Nazi war criminals in the dock for their crimes against humanity. Mercy does not preclude punishment.

Mercy was visible in a different form when President Gerald Ford pardoned his predecessor Richard Nixon. Ford's desire, as he said, was to end the "long national nightmare." Kate Anderson Brower points out *First in Line: Presidents, Vice Presidents and the Pursuit of Power*, the Nixons and Fords had been friends since their days together in the Congress. Ford, on one level, was moved by a sense of personal decency. Years later, in 2005, Ford admitted as much when he told Bob Woodward of the *Washington Post*, "I looked upon [Nixon] as my personal friend. And I always treasured our relationship. And I had no hesitancy about granting the pardon, because I felt that we had this relationship and that I didn't want to see my real friend have the stigma."[55]

Critics said Ford was giving Nixon a pass and some skeptics even believed that the price of Nixon giving up the presidency was the promise of a pardon. No evidence of that exists. Ford did find a measure of satisfaction in Nixon's acceptance of the pardon. Nixon admitted a degree of responsibility, saying that he was "wrong in not acting more decisively and more forthrightly in dealing with

Watergate, particularly when it reached the stage of judicial proceedings and grew from a political scandal into a national tragedy." This "imputation of guilt" stems from the 1915 Supreme Court Case, Burdick v. United States. Donald Rumsfeld, then Ford's chief of staff, wrote in his memoirs that Ford "kept a clipping of the Burdick case's ruling in his wallet."[56]

Ford himself did pay the price for his mercy. Two years later he lost a tightly contested election to Jimmy Carter. Historians believe that Ford's pardon of Nixon damaged him to a degree that made him vulnerable to defeat. Carter represented a fresh start and Ford himself, a merciful person, was tainted by his decision to show mercy to a fallen president. Ford himself did not regret the pardon and in doing so showed a spirit of grace—it's more about the giving than the taking.

Mercy in Conflict

Sometimes the desire to serve drives good people to make sacrifices for others. "The war against the hospitals is designed to break the will of the rebellion. But as long as some will fight for mercy, there is reason for all to hope." That is how Scott Pelley, correspondent for CBS's *60 Minutes*, signed off his program on the assistance that the Syrian American Medical Society is providing to casualties of the Syrian civil war.

The war is noted for its sheer brutality as troops loyal to Bashar Al Hassad take extreme measures to wipe out resistance, including the targeting of hospitals. "It's the worse humanitarian crisis of our lifetimes," Dr. Basel Termanini, a gastroenterologist from Steubenville, Ohio, said. The real heroes are the Syrian medical staffers who remain inside Syria despite the relentless conflict. "They know they risk in their lives, every day risking their family's life." They are the last line of medical assistance. The work is dangerous. More than 800 medical professionals have lost their lives trying to help the injured.

"Whatever they need," said Termanini, "we try to fulfill."

The Syrian America Medical Society has raised over $150 million in relief aid, which pays the salaries of Syrian staffers as well as provides relief services to other war-torn countries. SAM also co-ordinates the pro bono services of assisting physicians. Its physicians and staffers have delivered more than 100,000 babies and performed more than 400,000 surgeries.

Dr. Samer Attar from Chicago has volunteered to work in Syrian hospitals plying his craft as an orthopedic surgeon. Tamer Ghanem, a surgeon from Detroit, does facial reconstruction in a hospital located in Turkey on the border with Syria. These physicians have busy practices—not to mention safety at home in the U.S. but they feel the calling to serve others in war zones. Syrian medical staff told Dr. Samer, "that they would rather risk their lives dying in Syria trying to save lives than grow old comfortably from a distance watching the world fall apart." Samer feels similarly. "Twenty years from now, I didn't want to look back and say I wasn't a part of that." Despite the horror of man's inhumanity to man, you can find men and women willing to provide aid, even when it means endangering their own lives. Mercy, yes. Love—even more so.[57]

Forgiveness in the Face of Rage

Forgiveness is rooted in mercy, which is an attribute of grace. The ability to forgive someone who has done you wrong is an act of mercy. While there is an expectation of an apology for a transgression, forgiveness is an expression of mercy that does not demand it. Skip Prichard, veteran CEO and leadership author, grew up in a household where his parents, out of the goodness of their hearts, took in people who "were abused, addicted, abandoned." As a kid growing up, he thought all families did as his parents did. Growing up this way, Skip learned how to see people for who they really are rather than what they might seem. Once, as Skip told me, "my mom, Diane, was working with a young, troubled young lady who was taking classes at a beauty school. And my mom volunteered to have her haircut." The young woman, distraught and upset and seeking to provoke a confrontation, ended up shaving half of Diane's hair. It was not intended as a fashion statement; it was a venting of anger. His mother didn't blink. She simply stood up and gave the woman a hug. "It's okay, honey. I love you." The young lady broke down in tears. "What my mom recognized was 'I'm going to see the person inside you,'" Skip says. Diane met rage with love. "That's compassion," says Skip, "reacting in love when the expectation is you'd react in hatred and anger."

Acting on Compassion

Acting for the benefit of others is something that Mamadou Gassama did not contemplate in advance; it was something he did, almost automatically. Mamadou was walking down a Paris street minding his own business, as immigrants from Africa are wont to do when he heard a commotion and saw people pointing upwards. A 4-year old boy was dangling from a porch balcony four stories above the street.

Mamadou responded immediately and began climbing the outside face of the balconies. First floor, second floor, and then the third. Then with a powerful thrust upward he heaved himself up onto the fourth balcony and reached over and pulled the child who was still dangling precariously into his arms. The French dubbed him "Le Spider-Man" in honor of the action hero comic book character. A video of the daring rescue, filmed from street level, was posted online and went viral. Mamadou was quoted later as saying that the higher he climbed the more energy he gained. The crowd below was cheering, and their energy likely helped him heave himself upward floor by floor.

The courage Mamadou, age 22, showed in his climb may have been honed on his journey from Chad, years earlier, crossing the desert and eventually the Mediterranean Sea where he ended up in Italy. In 2018, he crossed illegally into France to join his brother, like so many of his fellow countryman who flee north to escape grinding poverty and periodic arm conflicts. Mamadou later spoke to reporters about the incident saying, "I saw all these people shouting, and cars sounding their horns. So, I crossed the road to go save him." Later after the child was safe, the effect of what he had done washed over him. "I started to shake, I could hardly stand up. I had to sit down."

One day later Mamadou was welcomed by French president, Emmanuel Macron, and awarded a gold medal for "courage and devotion." He was also granted "residency papers" that will allow him to work legally in France. Furthermore, he landed a job with the Paris firefighters where Macron said members were "eager to welcome" him. In addition, Macron invited Mamadou to apply for citizenship "because France is built on desire, and Mr. Gassama's commitment clearly showed that he has that desire." [58]

Compassionate Courage

"The courage of life," John F. Kennedy wrote in book *Profiles in Courage*, "is often less a dramatic spectacle than the courage of a final moment; but it is no less a magnificent mixture of triumph and tragedy." In his acceptance speech upon receiving the 2017 Profile in Courage Award, former President Barack Obama referenced President Kennedy and his family when he spoke about the role that courage plays in daily life. Obama recalled the late Senator Ted Kennedy telling him about the times when he would stroll the halls of the cancer ward when his son Teddy, Jr. was being treated in the seventies. While the elder Kennedy did not worry about paying for his son's treatment, this was not the case for so many other parents of children in the cancer ward. Parents did not complain; they simply did their best for their children. Courage requires endurance. And their courage inspired Ted Kennedy to devote his energies toward providing affordable health care.

"That's what the ordinary courage of everyday people can inspire when you're paying attention, the quiet sturdy courage of ordinary people doing the right thing day in and day out," said Obama. "They don't get attention for it. They don't seek it. They don't get awards for it. But that's what's defined America." Obama said he often saw courage in the example of men and women he met throughout his presidency. "We lose sight sometimes of our own obligations, each of ours, all the quiet acts of courage that unfold around us every single day, ordinary Americans who give something of themselves not for personal gain but for the enduring benefit of another."

Obama noted the courage of first responders and service men and women, but he noted a more universal demonstration of it. "The courage of a single mom who is working two jobs to make sure her kid can go to college. The courage of a small business owner who's keeping folks on the payroll because he knows the family relies on it, even if it's not always the right thing to do bottom line. The courage of somebody who volunteers to help some kids who need help." Courage then becomes less "a dramatic spectacle" than a daily act of giving, of sacrificing your time for the betterment of others.

Courage is inextricably linked to leadership because to lead others requires both the exultation of self as well as the sublimation of that same self. That is, you need to put yourself forward in order for others to follow and when you are in the lead you put their needs ahead of yourself. That requires courage certainly, one, to answer the call to lead, and two, to step aside as necessary. Courage, however, must have context. As President Kennedy once said, "Efforts and courage are not enough without purpose and direction." In other words, you need to apply courage—and the requisite effort—in order to accomplish something worthwhile. The application of purpose gives impetus as well as meaning to courage.[59]

While we apply the term courage to those we regard as heroes—and rightly so—we overlook the courage that it takes to face life's challenges. The nature of our human frailty dictates that sometimes we are spineless. We may back down when the boss challenges our ideas, or we may avoid having that painful but necessary conversation with a direct report. We may even take that "cowardice" with us home, avoiding similar talks with spouses, children, and parents. When we do so, we are negating our inner resourcefulness, our own inherent courage. Recognizing that flaw means we are aware, and with determination we can summon that strength when we need it. It just takes courage.

Gracious Courage

He was a man eleven months removed from the longest consecutive games played in a series in major league history. Yet as he shuffled, and with some assistance, to the microphone he seemed a pale shadow of his once commanding physique. His body drooped as if his powerful biceps and tree trunk-like thighs hung from his bones. He was the image of a spent man. Physically. Lou Gehrig, the Iron Horse, captain of the New York Yankees, the biggest ball club in the biggest city in America, leaned down and forward. His voice was hoarse, but it resonated with strength. He was back, if only for a moment, to enjoy the adulation of the New York fans who kept cheering. He was willing them to stop, but how? Then he spoke:

> Fans, for the past two weeks you have been reading about the bad break I got. Yet today I consider myself the luckiest man on the face of this earth. I have been in ballparks for seventeen years and have never received anything but kindness and encouragement from you fans.

Gehrig, gaunt and drawn, looked at everyone else but himself. He cited his owner and two managers.

Look at these grand men. Which of you wouldn't consider it the high-light of his career just to associate with them for even one day? Sure, I'm lucky. Who wouldn't consider it an honor to have known Jacob Ruppert? Also, the builder of baseball's greatest empire, Ed Barrow?

To have spent six years with that wonderful little fellow, Miller Huggins? Then to have spent the next nine years with that out-standing leader, that smart student of psychology, the best manager in baseball today, Joe McCarthy? Sure, I'm lucky.

Gehrig was always in the vernacular of the day, a good sport, citing here their cross-town National League rivals.

When the New York Giants, a team you would give your right arm to beat, and vice versa, sends you a gift—that's something. When everybody down to the groundskeepers and those boys in white coats remember you with trophies— that's something.

Gehrig made it personal. His own relationship with his mother was strained by his marriage. It was she who was overly controlling but Lou played it straight. And as author Richard Sandomir notes, it was Eleanor's mother, Mrs. Twitchell, who nursed him in his final months of life.

When you have a wonderful mother-in-law, who takes sides with you in squabbles with her own daughter—that's something. When you have a father and a mother who work all their lives, so you can have an education and build your body—it's a blessing.

And this is as personal as it gets. Eleanor Gehrig was the love of his life.

When you have a wife, who has been a tower of strength and shown more courage than you dreamed existed—that's the finest I know.

Historians debate about how much Gehrig knew about his condition. On this day, however, he was looking ahead.

So, I close in saying that I may have had a tough break, but I have an awful lot to live for.

When the speech, given impromptu and without notes, was done, Gehrig slipped from the field and back down into the Yankee clubhouse, never to set foot on a major league baseball diamond again. The day was hot, and Gehrig said later he was soaking wet with sweat. He died two years later on June 2, 1941 of amyotrophic lateral sclerosis (ALS), or simply, "Lou Gehrig's disease."

Complete recordings of the speech do not exist, and newsreel footage is incomplete. And as Richard Sandomir points out in his book, *The Pride of the Yankees: Lou Gehrig, Gary Cooper and the Making of a Classic*, in the movie that immortalized Gehrig for the ages, sportswriters felt free to summarize what he had said, sometimes faithfully, sometimes not. And for that reason, some of the names of players he cited are omitted.

You can tell a good deal about a man when he's facing his end and Gehrig's moment of farewell was less about him than about his experiences and all the good things he had experienced in baseball from his days at Columbia University to stardom with the Yankees.

Gehrig even served for a time, after the Yankees, as a labor commissioner for the City of New York. Appointed by Mayor Fiorello LaGuardia, Gehrig counseled—what we would today call "at risk youth." One man who was sent to see him was none other than Rocky Graziano, then a two-bit punk with a criminal record. Whether Gehrig set him straight is conjecture, but years later

Graziano became the heavyweight boxing champion of the world and retired undefeated. Kindness is an example, and even under duress, it becomes more evident.[60]

There is a curious backstory that Richard Sandomir tells about Gary Cooper on a USO tour to entertain troops in the South Pacific. The year was 1943 and the fighting on the islands that Cooper visited was intense. While GIs, of course, wanted to see the starlets in the show, when Cooper visited New Guinea, one soldier called out to Cooper to do the "Luckiest Man" speech. Others, who had seen *The Pride of the Yankees,* echoed the GI's request. Cooper, ever the obliging star, asked for a moment to recollect his lines; it had been a year and a half since he had filmed the speech. He scribbled some notes and gave his rendition. It was so popular that Cooper repeated it at all his stops, including a culminating show at the Royal Theatre in Sydney, Australia.

There was, as Sandomir writes, something in the words of a dying man looking at his end without rancor, choosing instead to focus on the positive things and life in the future that resonated with the troops fighting far from home in a forgotten corner of the world. Cooper/Gehrig reminded them of what they were fighting for in the Pacific, and if luck would have it, enjoy once again stateside.

Compassion at the VA

Many of those then young GIs who Cooper met overseas would one day find themselves in old age under treatment in a Veteran's Administration hospital. Kindness extends to all parts of life, including its parting. Dr. Sanjay Saint, a clinical professor of internal medicine at the University of Michigan who also serves as Chief of Medicine at the Ann Arbor VA Medical Center, wrote a moving essay about the Final Salute, the process of acknowledging the passing of a veteran.

After the family is called for a final visit, the body is put on a gurney and draped with the flag. Taps sound over the PA system. It is "the signal for the health care workers, and, especially, their fellow soldiers, to come to the doors of their rooms. Civilians stand with their hands on their hearts. Veterans give the military salute, standing if they are able."

Dr. Saint continues, "Rituals and ceremonies are important links to the past, and they are reminders of what it takes to improve tomorrow." "Being a VA doctor gives me pride, no more so than when I watch how our VA honors those veterans who have died." Dr. Saint cites Abraham Lincoln's insistence on treating veterans as he said in his Second Inaugural Address, "To care for him who shall have borne the battle and for his widow, and his orphan." Dr. Saint notes that when he was in medical school, his patients at the VA were veterans from World War I. Now it's those from World War II as well as Korea, Vietnam, Iraq, and Afghanistan. And most of his colleagues feel "inspired by those [veterans] who entrust us with their care and their lives."[61]

Giving While Suffering

David Feherty is another person who devotes service to those in uniform. Feherty is one of the funniest storytellers—certainly the funniest former PGA Tour pro—you will find on television. And he's on television a great deal since he works as a golf analyst for NBC Sports and does a series of shows for the Golf Channel. His patter is insightful as well as "rolling on the floor" funny, which hides part of his personality.

Feherty is also a recovering alcoholic who mourns daily the loss of his son, Shey, who died from alcohol and cocaine consumption at age 29. The son had spiraled out of control and Feherty had been advised to keep his distance, at least financially, as a means of helping him find sobriety. And as is the case with so many parents who lose children to addiction, he blames himself.

Feherty is very open with his own struggles. In his first season of *Feherty*, he told the story of his daughter offering to bring him a bottle of Bushmill's whisky, asking him with childhood innocence, "What are you addicted to?" Golf Channel president Mike Mc-Carley recalls the moment the show aired, "That's when we really started to get a lot of letters and emails from addicts, from people who didn't really think there were shows on television with people like them. That's when we knew we were really striking a chord that was greater than golf."

An insightful *Golf Digest* profile of Feherty, written by sportswriter and best-selling author, John Feinstein, captures Feherty's wit as well as his pain. What resonates clearly is Feherty's willingness to be there for others. Fellow Northern Ireland golfer and close friend, Rory McIlroy says, "David does best when he's thinking about anything but David. It's why he's so good with helping others but struggles at times to help himself."

Feherty credits his second wife, Anita, whom he married in 1996, for saving him from drink and drugs. He was trying to raise his two sons and not functioning well at all. He was so thin she thought he might be HIV positive. It took him more than a decade of trying to embrace sobriety. She manages his career, including his finances. She says this about him: "I think that his genuine kindness has given him a few mulligans in life, more than most people get."

Feherty regularly entertains the troops; his surviving son is in the Texas National Guard and has been deployed to combat zones. Beginning in 2005, Feherty's work with veterans echoes his roots. "I grew up in Northern Ireland—it was a war zone," he says. "There were troops on the street. They were fighting an enemy that hid behind women and children, that wouldn't wear a uniform. Sectarian murders, bombs going off, it all seems familiar to me, the war in Iraq." With Rick Kell, he founded the Troops First Foundation. His efforts are appreciated. In 2013 the Army awarded Feherty the U.S. Army's Outstanding Civilian Service Award."

Feherty's support network includes three former presidents, Barack Obama, George W. Bush, and Bill Clinton, who reminded him that he was a great dad, which he knew, and he wanted to offer, "anything he could to help." Golf legend Tom Watson was the one who finally convinced Feherty to give up alcohol. Watson, also in recovery, said he saw himself in the younger man. As quick-witted as Feherty is, he prefers the company of himself. Yet he goes on stage regularly with his two-hour standup comedy gig. Stage fright is never far away. He told Feinstein over the course of his show, he has lost his pace, saying, "Totally frozen and unable to go on? Close, but no. Not yet." Feherty in a way was born to entertain. He had studied opera with the possibility of performing professionally. He chose golf where his wit and charm endeared him to fellow pros and the public.

And, while he suffers from depression and bi-polarity, Feherty puts himself out there for others. The reason his friends are loyal to him is that he is loyal to them. And his capacity for doing good for others—despite his pain—means he serves as an example for others.[62]

"Being Hope"

One of the leaders I interviewed for this book—Dave Johnson—knows what it is like to live with the pain—like Feherty—of losing his son. As Dave, a former nurse and family therapist, told me, "I think there comes a time and space in our lifetime where we recognize that hope is not esoteric, it's very tangible, it's concrete and it's within each of us, our ability to be intentional about being an anchor for someone during a time of need." Dave put his thoughts into an essay he titled, "Being Hope."

> *In my youth, I felt like I didn't have enough life experience to give what was needed. As I aged, I experienced enough of my own trauma that I feared I would grow cynical. I am not a violent person, but I recall punching a wall one day after hearing a story about the death*

of a child. It was too close to my own heart, having lost my oldest son, Justin, to cancer. I cried at our staffing (a meeting of therapists to help ourselves stay grounded by reviewing new clients) that day. "How can I bring hope?" I would often ponder. The last thing folks in healthcare or counseling need is a Pollyanna-ish, "The sun will come out tomorrow" or likeminded cliché. How could a counselor, friend, parent, sibling, spouse, confidant, etc. provide an anchor in a life storm to someone in need?"

Dave answers his question with these words: "I believe it's by being hope." Manifesting hope for Dave means cultivating it personally and then sharing it with others. Dave argues that to develop hope you must do four things: one, protect it; two, cultivate it through mindfulness; three, invite hope; and four, deliver hope. In this way, we nurture the hope within ourselves. And doing so enables us to share it with others.

Hope is essential to our lives:

"We all need the antidote of hope. Hope for our personal family, community, and world well-being. Hope truly is a big word. When we feel lost, confused, grief-stricken, ill or immobilized by fear, it is hope that anchors our soul and bridges us to new land, dreams and a brighter future."

Dave also believes in a connection between hope and grace because both require the sense of presence, the investment of self into the life of another. "Grace is probably the energetic field of hope," as he told me. "I can feel it, there's an energy that moves around and around and around and you can sense it," he said.

Dave Johnson tells a story from when he was sixteen and working as an orderly. Responding to an emergency call in the hospital, he saw a teenager who was bleeding profusely. "My eyes joined hers, and when I peered into her eyes, I saw something that I'd never seen before. It was despair, it was hopelessness." The girl had cut herself in an attempt to end her life. But as her eyes met Dave's, she calmed down, and later Dave spent time with her while she was being treated in the emergency room.

Flash forward thirty-seven years. Dave is driving down a country road in Indiana and stops at a yard sale. There was a glass bowl he was interested in purchasing that he thought would look good in his garden. As he was considering the purchase, a woman about his age approached him and called him his name. "You were my nurse. And you saved my life," she said. Dave, of course, was not yet a nurse back then but as he says now, "It's synchronicity. I looked into her eyes again, and they were joy-filled, and they were good, and they were kind. I don't know that I changed her life trajectory as much as she changed mine . . . If you're truly present with people, they respond. So, we're vessels of hope, we're beacons of light, I mean those are all metaphors to interpret, but it's the eyes" that reveal the inner self.[63]

Compassion as Gratitude

Revealing our inner selves enables us to be more open and giving to others. "Gratitude is like cholera" is the opening line from "Be More Grateful," a chapter in Chris Lowney's book, *Make Today Matter: 10 Habits for a Better Life (and World.)* "Both are highly contagious, potent and spread person to person," Lowney writes. "But cholera induces death, gratitude induces happiness." A former Jesuit seminarian turned investment banker, Lowney knows something about disease having lived abroad, including in some of the poorest parts of the world.

It was in his corporate career, however, that one lesson in gratitude resonates. It was an email from his boss thanking him for the good work he had done on a project. Lowney (whom I interviewed for this book) confesses he read and re-read that email multiple times throughout the year; it always gave him the get-up-and-go he needed, especially when confronting obstacles—human and otherwise.

Gratitude, as a topic, is *au courant*. You will find it embedded in self-help books, plastered on posters, and tweeted throughout cyberspace. And rightly so! Gratitude is the grease that makes working with others easier; it dampens the sparks that occur when co-workers rub each other the wrong way.

Gratitude can be defined in two parts: external and internal. Let's take external because I think it is the easier of the two to master. Why? Because it is action oriented. We counsel those in authority to make certain to thank those who report to them.

That simple recognition can take the form of a year-end bonus (which is what Lowney also received with his thank you note) or a simple email. More importantly the gratitude you show to others must be sincere. It would be tempting to say, "from the heart," but since management structures are "heartless," the challenge is to keep the affirmation real.

Settle for a direct and frank appreciation. Make it known how much you value an individual's contributions. Be as specific as possible. Delineate what the individual has done to receive a thank you and tell him or her how much his or her work is appreciated. Simple words certainly, but they go a long way. All of us cherish moments of authentic recognition.[64]

There are tangible benefits to gratitude. According to a study by Robert A. Emmons and Michael E. McCullough, respondents who felt gratitude had a more positive outlook on life. The authors concluded that "a conscious focus on blessings may have emotional and interpersonal benefits." Sam Walker, writing in the *Wall Street Journal*, cited this study as well as a 2012 study from John Templeton Foundation that reported "a majority of people believe gratitude pays dividends at work. Of those surveyed, 71% said they'd feel better about themselves if their boss expressed more gratitude for their efforts, while 81% said they would work harder."

Cheryl Baker of Give and Take, Inc. (whom we met in Chapter 3) cited research from the Royal Society of Open Science that when people ask for help, they receive it, some 80% of the time. Baker notes however that less than 6% of those who receive assistance say thank you. As Baker notes, "It's great that people are inclined to help when asked [but] troublesome that givers are so rarely thanked." To make her point, Baker cited ten benefits to "expressing thanks." For example, when employees are thanked, according to research conducted by the University of Pennsylvania' Wharton School of Business, productivity increased. A 2014 study that appeared in the journal *Emotion* noted that people feel more connected when they are thanked. And as an *Applied Psychology: Health and Well-Being* article reported from a 2011 study, "grateful people sleep better. Other studies say when people are thanked, they tend to be physically and mentally healthy, find greater satisfaction at work, and demonstrate higher levels of self-esteem, including the lowering of negative emotions such as "aggression and jealousy." This clearly tells us that expressing gratitude benefits not only the receiver but the giver.[65]

The second definition of gratitude may be trickier to master because it deals with our inner selves. We humans are adept at fooling ourselves. We can go through the motions like circus acrobats, hurling through life without seeming to miss a step or a hand-off, when in reality we are missing everything. Why? We have deadened ourselves to the joy that comes from recognizing ourselves as people who belong to other people—at work, at home, in our community.

Gratitude then is the recognition that you have something to offer the world and the world has something to offer you. Lowney quotes Cicero, the great Roman orator, who wrote, "Gratitude is not only the greatest of all virtues, but the parent of all." The old Roman, who gave his life for the Republic, was right. If you cannot feel gratitude, you cannot *feel* overall, and if you cannot *sense* then you cannot exert courage, demonstrate integrity, or show love. For one simple reason, you lack the capacity to care.

By contrast, gratitude is that capacity to care. We need to reframe our lives with a constant awareness of just how important feeling gratitude within ourselves is, because it actually helps our overall well-being.

It's important to acknowledge that you have something to offer and you can deliver. From that recognition comes the thanks you need to be grateful—for who you are and what you have. "Make gratitude your attitude" may look good plastered on a poster or sent via Twitter but it's not enough to say it, you need to live it —outside and in![66]

COMPASSION IS THE REFLECTION OF NEED IN OTHERS AND THE DESIRE WITHIN US TO HELP.

Compassion: What the Leaders Say

Compassion is an expression of grace that puts the needs of the other before the needs of the self.

***

"Compassion is understanding people in their context and helping them from where they are," says Mike McKinney. "Compassionate leaders focus on the culture because they see the connection between individuals and individual problems and the environment people are in."

Scott Moorehead builds on the idea of the right environment. "To me, there's a continuum here that starts with caring. And you have to allow a system where people will care. And then ultimately, you have to teach people empathy. So, empathy is the continuation of caring ... Once you cease focusing on yourself and feel what someone else feels then you've experienced empathy. But then the continuation of empathy is compassion, which is where you've experienced empathy, and now you're absolutely called to do something about it."

For Alaina Love, one cannot demonstrate compassion without self-awareness. "When you can connect with your own true feelings and be honest with yourself about them, the good, the bad, and the

ugly, then you develop a muscle. And that muscle allows you to understand and feel compassion for others when they're going through
a challenging time. And as you practice that muscle strength and
your ability to show up for the other person gets stronger."

Chris Lowney agrees. "Whenever I'm irritated by somebody,
I try to say to myself . . . "I understand there's something going on
inside you that makes you behave in a way that is irritating me right
now,'" Recognizing one's own limited sense of patience can be the
means of connecting with others. "The reality is I can be compassionate and loving but still understand that there are times when I
have to do something that's going to be unpopular or difficult for
you to accept."

Skip Prichard grew up in a home where compassion was a way
of life. His parents took into their home people in need. "Wherever
you were from, all ages, all races, all types of people, and they were
all troubled. They were abused, addicted, abandoned. And it was an
incredibly way to live. It was an incredibly way to grow up . . . And
some people stayed for a day. And some people stayed with us for
years."

"Compassion is energy as well, it's as soft, it's tender, it's loving,
it's kind," says Dave Johnson. He associates it with the imagery of a
mother soothing a baby as she sways that child from right to left or
left to right, the movement, the motion is kind and gentle. She may
sing, she may touch, but it's a movement, and so I see compassion as
movement as well."

"Compassion is an intrinsic motivation you act on," says Tim
Sanders "That intrinsic motivation is that others in your life do not
suffer unnecessarily. What I think of in terms of showing compassion
as a leader is reducing unnecessary suffering."

Stephen M.R. Covey views compassion as a combination of
empathy and understanding. It is also the willingness to endure
suffering with someone else. "We suffer with the person. We walk
with them. We sacrifice with them. We mourn with them. We love

them." It is part of what Stephen calls "the journey" of "walking with them" through an experience, through their lives

***

Think about these questions:

- What does it mean to have compassion?

- What happens when compassion is ignored?

- How can you channel your passion for purpose towards compassion for others?

- What does the concept of mercy mean to you? How could you practice it?

- How can you show forgiveness toward others?

- How do we show gratitude toward our colleagues?

- How can we put ourselves second when it comes to serving other? Is it possible? Why?

Graceful Leadership Steps

Compassion—*regarding the dignity of others as worthwhile*

- Focus your passion for life into compassion for others.

- Discuss with friends how you can collaborate on community activities.

- Find ways to eliminate "distances" that divide you from people with whom you disagree.

- Frame problems as opportunities to learn rather than occasions of blame.

- Look at others as people not as objects, that is, as people, like yourself, worthy of interest.

- Seek examples of people you admire for giving back to others. Ask yourself how they do it? What can you do to emulate their example?

- Condemn evil but withhold judgment of the perpetrator until you know the circumstance.

"I am going to use all my energies to develop myself, to expand my heart out to others; to achieve enlightenment for the benefit of all beings. I am going to have kind thoughts towards others, I am not going to get angry or think badly about others. I am going to benefit others as much as I can."

—Dalai Lama XIV

Energy

E is energy, *the spirit that catalyzes us.*

Get up and go—that's energy. It is the vitality that animates our purpose translating what we want to do into what we actually do. Energy is a kind of caffeine that revs our internal motor so that we can stay the course when times are tough as well as enjoy the course when things are going well. Energy is the spunk of life. And it is swell.

Energy to serve

Few people—with perhaps the exceptions of George Washington upon the nation's founding and Abraham Lincoln upon the nation's possible dissolution—have tackled the office of the Presidency in such a crisis as Franklin Delano Roosevelt. And he did so with boundless enthusiasm and energy.

Roosevelt's mantra during his momentous first one hundred days was this statement: "Do something. If it works, do more of it. If it doesn't, do something else." And with good reason, the nation Roosevelt was elected to lead was nearly prostrate. One-fifth of the workforce was unemployed, banks were nearly insolvent, businesses were collapsing. Historian Jon Meacham in *The Soul of America* cites that dark forces were brewing abroad that advocated state control, either communist or fascist. Democracy was cracking, and people were afraid.

And so, when FDR made his inaugural address on March 4, 1933, he said the "only thing we have to fear is fear itself." There, in one short statement, the president laid bare the boogeyman at the door. Quiet, nameless, but so terrible in scope! *Fear.* Roosevelt with his customary upbeat style and strong voice laid bare that fear and set the nation on a course toward recovery.

As historian and journalist Jonathan Alter writes in *The Defining Moment,* "That March of 1933, the new president did not have to mobilize aging members of the American Legion under martial law. Franklin Roosevelt mobilized himself and his talent for leadership. He found his voice, and his voice defined America." During those Hundred Days, he employed his executive authority to put the banks on holiday (not closing, mind you, but a holiday), set up an "alphabet soup" of agencies, and set about finding ways to put people back to work. For once the people had hope and they found it in the papers but mostly at their radios where Roosevelt would serenade them with his plans—labeled fireside chats—that talked about what his plans for the future were.

It was his voice—arched and patrician befitting his social class and Groton-Harvard pedigree—that provided comfort. He was also out and about visiting people where they lived and worked. No one seemed to mind that the man in whom they had placed their hopes for the future was himself a man who depended upon the aide of others for his daily routine. Stricken with polio at age 39, he wore heavy leg braces to stand and required the aid of others to walk.

But it was in his paralysis that historians, particularly James Tobin, whose book *The Man He Became: How FDR Defied Polio to Win the Presidency*, argue that his illness was what gave him his common touch. Although he was to the manor born, as a man recovering from polio he worked hard to recover and spent as much time as possible in Warm Springs, Georgia in its mineral baths. He eventually bought the place and turned it into a sanitarium for fellow polio victims.

What animated Roosevelt throughout his presidency was restoring America to its principles in ways that enable the able-bodied to work and the less fortunate to find relief. Called a traitor to his class, he reveled in upsetting the order of the day in his quest to do it all. As FDR once said, "The test of our progress is not whether we add more to the abundance of those who have much; it is whether we provide enough for those who have too little." Never did that voice resonate more clearly than on the evening of D-Day, June 6, 1944, when President Franklin Roosevelt addressed the nation. Rather than give a report on the invasion, Roosevelt invoked his adaptation of a prayer taken from the Anglican Book of Common Prayer, a favorite of his.

> *Almighty God: Our sons, pride of our Nation, this day have set upon a mighty endeavor, a struggle to preserve our Republic, our religion, and our civilization, and to set free a suffering humanity.*

> *Lead them straight and true; give strength to their arms, stoutness to their hearts, steadfastness in their faith.*

Roosevelt mentions the word "grace" once in the address and it is in passing but his remarks focus on the spirit of what the word implies.

They will need Thy blessings. Their road will be long and hard. For the enemy is strong. He may hurl back our forces. Success may not come with rushing speed, but we shall return again and again; and we know that by Thy grace, and by the righteousness of our cause, our sons will triumph.

Even with grace comes suffering and sacrifice.

They will be sore tried, by night and by day, without rest–until the victory is won. The darkness will be rent by noise and flame. Men's souls will be shaken with the violences of war.

Roosevelt emphasizes the nature of those who fight and honor their cause.

For these men are lately drawn from the ways of peace. They fight not for the lust of conquest. They fight to end conquest. They fight to liberate. They fight to let justice arise, and tolerance and good will among all Thy people. They yearn but for the end of battle, for their return to the haven of home.

Roosevelt contrasts the righteous cause of the Allies with the evil forces of the Nazis.

With Thy blessing, we shall prevail over the unholy forces of our enemy. Help us to conquer the apostles of greed and racial arrogancies. Lead us to the saving of our country, and with our sister Nations into a world unity that will spell a sure peace, a peace invulnerable to the schemings of unworthy men.

For Roosevelt a better tomorrow was always the intention.

And a peace that will let all of men live in freedom, reaping the just
rewards of their honest toil.
Thy will be done, Almighty God.

While acknowledging the power of the Almighty, Roosevelt, ever cognizant that he was the president and not a pastor, was careful to focus his words on the purpose of the cause —uprooting a tyrannical power. For Roosevelt the cause was sacred, but it would not be waged with words. It was fought with the blood and treasure of the nation and its Allies. Peace could only be possible through the hard effort of sacrifice touched with the power of grace. In the Christian tradition, grace is not earned; it is given. As such men and women must use it not for personal enrichment but for the good of all.

The many years in office—coupled with chronic heart disease—took their toll on Roosevelt. In the last year of his life, some noted he looked more ghost-like than human and that is where his energy morphed into sheer determination. He wanted to have a hand in shaping the post-War world and he pushed hard for the establishment of a United Nations. In February of 1945 just two months before his death, he travelled 14,000 miles round-trip to meet with Winston Churchill and Josef Stalin in Yalta on the Black Sea, an arduous trip in an era before jet travel.

Such determination was a hallmark of Roosevelt's courage. Jon Meacham notes that Churchill, his ally in arms during World War II, praised Roosevelt to Parliament after FDR's death in April 1945:

"President Roosevelt's physical affliction lay heavily upon him. It
was a marvel that he bore up against it through all the many years
of tumult and storm. Not one man in ten millions, stricken and crip
pled as he was, would have attempted to plunge into a life of physical

and mental exertion and of hard, ceaseless political controversy. Not one in ten millions would have tried, not one in a generation would have succeeded, not only in entering this sphere, not only in acting vehemently in it, but in becoming indisputable master of the scene."

Roosevelt was no saint. He strayed in his marriage. He also sought to pack the Supreme Court with political stalwarts and perhaps worst of all, he signed an executive order than interned over 100,000 Japanese Americans at the start of World War II. Yet his better self-prevailed in what he accomplished by shepherding the nation through a catastrophic depression and a global war that saw some 12 million Americans in military service. Satisfaction for Roosevelt can be summed up in this quote of his: "Happiness lies in the joy of achievement and the thrill of creative effort." Confident, energetic, and focused on doing something positive, in 1932 he was labeled the Happy Warrior, a label he wore as proudly as his smile.[67]

Renewable Energy

Christine Porath, a professor at Georgetown who studies workplace civility, told me that unlike time, energy is a renewable resource, "fuel for high-performance." The challenge is to find ways to renew it. For Roosevelt energy came from addressing challenges of the day; the bigger the problem, the greater his ability to rally himself to fight the good fight.

The idea of renewability has roots in an article that psychologist, Jim Loehr, and author, Tony Schwartz, wrote about in "The Corporate Athlete" for *Harvard Business Review* in 2001. Executives need to learn how to develop and renew their sources of energy that come in three types: physical, emotional, and spiritual. When these aspects are in balance, individuals can perform better than they can when one or more of these aspects are depleted.

Tony Schwartz, now CEO and President of The Energy

Project, which helps individuals and teams use their energies wisely and constructively, notes in a subsequent post for *Harvard Business Review* that many senior executives feel they don't have the energy to do their jobs effectively. Schwartz, co-author of *The Power of Full Engagement* and *The Way We're Working Isn't Working*, and his team have developed The Energy Audit, a self-assessment that can help individuals assess their energy levels. By identifying where they are lacking, they can focus on how to improve.

Their research showed that a majority of executives had "trouble focusing on one thing at a time," did not have enough "time to think strategically and creatively," and also found themselves becoming "impatient, frustrated or irritable at work." Reasons for this dissatisfaction as Schwartz's research reveals, come from lack of sleep, lack of exercise, eating lunch at their desks and not spending time with family or having "too little time for the activities they most deeply enjoy."

Obvious areas of improvement come from three sources: eating properly, sleeping sufficiently, exercising for fitness, and making time for family and self. These activities help individuals feel better about themselves and improve their overall levels of energy.[68]

Christine Porath approaches energy from the perspective of the mind. Meditating can improve mental acuity as well as energy. Using techniques of breath control, those who meditate can find ways to link their thought processes to their daily activities. Yoga, too, can facilitate meditation because it combines breathing with physical movement. Meditation complements mindfulness, which is the ability to be present in the moment. It requires discipline to be mindful and that's where meditation helps. Mindfulness improves a sense of awareness both of self and the situation. As such, mindfulness can help us pay attention to what's important and disregard what is extraneous. Easy to say, but difficult to practice!

Passion Fuels Energy

Once Willie Nelson was so ill that when he got on stage he could not sing. Disgusted, he threw his hat into the audience and left the stage. He had a bad case of the flu, but he was determined to persevere, although he simply could not. His wife said she was worried. And why wouldn't she? After all Willie Nelson, the legend himself was 85 years old. Most men his age do not travel the country playing on stage. Fortunately, Willie had his family with him.

"We went to Maui," Willie's wife, Annie D'Angelo, told David Greene on NPR's *Fresh Air*, "He got some fresh air, but it took a good month," she says. "Then, he was a little nervous about it, but I heard him singing so I knew he was fine. He would sneak off in the music room and sing and pick." When he recovered—as his song says—he went "back on the road again." The question of energy naturally arises, and while his body might have faltered—temporarily—his spirit did not.

My grandmother, herself, an accomplished pianist, used to say that great musicians live long because their music keeps them going. She was referring to musicians such as conductor, Arturo Toscanini; cellist, Pablo Casals; pianists, Vladimir Horowitz, and Arthur Rubinstein. But she might have been speaking about Willie as well as his sister, Bobbie, who is two years older and plays piano in his band.

Like most musicians and entertainers, the energy comes from performing, "Just the last two shows have just blown my mind," said son Lukas. "We're playing really good music and Dad is singing his ass off." To which Willie added, "There's nothing that makes a parent happier than having your kids up there doing things with you, especially if they're good." Energy is renewable when you do what you love doing.[69]

What keeps musicians going is a passion for what they do. Alaina Love, an author and business leader, believes energy revolves around passion. According to Alaina's years of research on purpose, passion, and fulfillment, the passions exhibited by a person are the outward expression of the deeper purpose that drives them. These passions can be categorized into 10 specific "archetypes" or styles, that each carry an energy signature which others can perceive. Some folks, with a Builder archetype, for example, "exhibit a 'get it done, accomplishment-focused, I'm-in-charge" energy. Others, such as "Healers, Altruists, Teachers, and Connectors" manifest a type of energy that "invites others in because individuals with these archetypes are empathic, socially conscious, avid learners, and open to sharing, respectively." Individuals with these archetypes thrive by being in a relationship with others.

Since Alaina's research also indicates that we each have three main archetypes as dominant within our personality, the challenge is for us to understand the energy of each of those passions and how they may be influencing the way in which we are perceived by others. Armed with that understanding, we're in a better position to align our intent in our interactions with others to the impact that we most desire to achieve from those interactions.[70]

De-Energizing Behavior

Part of seeking to nurture energy is to stay positive. There is a sign on a door of the office of Pope Francis with the headline that says, "No Whining." The sign was a gift from Dr. Salvo Noe, a psychologist and motivational speaker. On his website Dr. Noe posted a picture of himself giving the sign to the Pope who laughed when he read it. The sign, written by Dr. Noe in Italian, reads:

> *Violators are subject to a syndrome of always feeling like a victim and the consequent reduction of your sense of humor and capacity to solve problems . . . Stop complaining and take steps to improve your life.*

The Pope is addressing a situation that bugs many executives—underlings who do little but complain. Good bosses don't stand for naysayers. Here's some advice for the next time you bring a problem to your boss. Don't! Here is what you can do instead:

Identify the problem. Inform your boss about the situation and tell him or her why it is a problem. Don't make yourself the object of the story. Talk about why the issue or problem is hurting the team.

Offer a solution. Suggest what you can do to remedy the situation. Be specific and prescriptive.

Gain agreement as to what to do next. Get permission to implement your idea, or have the boss make the decision about what to do next.

Following these steps may not bring immediate relief but it will demonstrate to your boss that you are not a whiner. You are a problem solver. Organizations need people who are willing to think for themselves. At the same time, before you act you need to get permission. Otherwise, you will create bigger problems. Complaining is inherent in the human condition—especially in times of doubt or fear. At a general audience, Pope Francis once said, God "is a father and this is a form of prayer. Complain to the Lord, this is good." Complain to your boss, no![71]

Collaboration as Learning

Complaining to colleagues drains energy, and energy is essential to successful teamwork. The holy grail of teamwork is collaboration. When two or more people can put their ideas together to create something better than themselves, wonderful things happen, be it a new business, a better process, or even a work of art. Essential to teaming is a sublimation of ego. You put yours aside so that you can listen to someone else's ideas. Your ego never goes away, nor should it, but you tone it down to be open to something else: learning.

And so, it was with that thought in mind that I discovered "10 Rules for Students and Teachers." Sister Corita Kent, an influential artist and educator, was the original author of "The 10 Rules." Composer John Cage popularized them and had them posted for students at the Merce Cunningham Studio. Merce, a renowned choreographer, was Cage's collaborator and romantic partner.

Themes in the "10 Rules" revolve around trust as well as the push to get everything you can out of an experience. Self-discipline is important as the need to follow a leader when necessary. At the same time, it is necessary to break the rules so that you can seek what Sister Corita calls "X qualities." Sister Corita advises students "not to try and create and analyze at the same time. They are different processes." That very wise thought gets to the heart of brainstorming. You generate but do not critique. Go for the flow. This certainly helps when initiating a project. There will be plenty of time for criticism. Go for the creative and see where it takes you.

As an addendum to the "10 Rules," Sister Corita added Helpful Hints. While each could be its own rule, my feeling is that Sister Corita intended them as pieces of advice. For example, she advises students to absorb all the experiences around them, including going to movies as well as to class. The first Helpful Hint is most relevant for anyone seeking to collaborate. "Always Be Around." The best teammates practice that mantra. They don't clock in mentally because their clock is always ticking. They are ready and available. They alternate between being creative and constructive, challenging, and supportive. Most important their authority comes from their presence. The best teammates are invested in the project, so people respect their contribution.

Sister Corita's final note, written all in caps, is *SAVE EVERYTHING*. As Sister Corita advises, "Something may come in handy later." So true! A rejected idea for one project may metamorphose into a great idea for another project. Or more often, the idea may combine with a colleague or two's ideas, which can lead to something even better. Collaboration is both art and practice. It is creative in that it is generative. It is practice because, as Sister Corita advises, you need discipline. And there is something else that comes from strong collaboration. Joy. "Be happy when you can manage it." As Sister Corita says, "Enjoy yourself. It is lighter than you think."[72]

Joy, Joy, Joy

Sister Corita understood that working with others—collaborating with them for improvement—is joyful. Joy is an element of grace. Putting grace to good use for others does engender feelings of joy; you feel good about doing something positive. There is satisfaction in working for the greater good for an individual or a community. While much of this book is focused on what grace does for others, it also enriches the individual who gives. Giving brings joy to oneself. And when you feel joy, you feel good about the world, happy even. Real happiness comes from feeling a kind of oneness with the world and those in it. It does not come from things. While buying something special—a house, a car, a new gadget—produces delight, but such delight is fleeting. Real happiness comes from giving to another.

Peggy Noonan, columnist for the *Wall Street Journal* and former speechwriter for Ronald Reagan, unearthed a television interview that famed CBS correspondent Mike Wallace did with Oscar Hammerstein, the award-winning lyricist and librettist of many Broadway hits, including *Oklahoma*, *South Pacific* and *The King and I*. When Wallace asked Hammerstein about his work being overly "sentimental," Hammerstein replied with a wry soliloquy about sophistication. "The sophisticate is a man who thinks he can swim better than he can and sometimes drowns himself. He thinks he can drive better than he really can and sometimes causes great smash-ups." Hammerstein then summed up his feelings. "So, in my book there's nothing wrong with sentiment because the things we're sentimental about are the fundamental things in life, the birth of a child, the death of a child, or of anybody, falling in love. I couldn't be anything but sentimental about these basic things."

Hammerstein demurred when asked about sentimentality. "When a writer writes anything about anything at all, he gives himself away." For example, South Pacific deals with the love affair between an American sailor and a Polynesian woman. In Hammerstein's view, "all this prejudice that we have is something that fades away in the face of something that's really important." (Which Noonan labels as "love.") Furthermore, in *The King and I*—featuring a Welsh school-teacher in the Kingdom of Siam— "all race and color had faded in their getting to know and love each other." Viewed through the lens of the 21st century, Hammerstein's ideas may seem anachronistic. For the mid-20th century, they were groundbreaking.

Hammerstein told a story about a cop in New York who stopped him for jaywalking. Expecting to get a ticket, the cop instead complimented the lyricist on his work. He also asked him if he were religious. Hammerstein answered, "Well, I don't belong to any church." Referring to the cop he said, "and then he patted me on the back, and he said, 'Ah, you're religious all right.'" Hammerstein realized that he was religious after all. The cop "had discovered from the words of my songs that he had faith—faith in mankind, faith that there was something more powerful than mankind behind it all, and faith that in the long run good triumphs over evil. "If that's religion, I'm religious, and it is my definition of religion," Hammerstein said.

Hammerstein practiced his good behavior. He was a mentor to Stephen Sondheim, a friend of Hammerstein's son, James. When he was in high school, Sondheim showed Hammerstein a musical entitled *By George*, which he had written for their school play, expecting to receive a heap of praise. Hammerstein did one better; he gave him constructive criticism. "But if you want to know why it's terrible, I'll tell you," said Hammerstein. Sondheim later said, "In that afternoon I learned more about songwriting and the musical theater than most people learn in a lifetime."

Recognizing the seriousness of his protégé, Hammerstein

challenged Sondheim to write four different musicals, each one based on different sources—a play, a novel and something original. Two were eventually produced, *All the Glitters* and *Climb High.* Over the years Sondheim emerged with his own unmistakable voice. Sondheim wrote lyrics for *West Side Story* before writing the score and lyrics for a number of ground-breaking Broadway shows including *Follies, A Little Night Music, Sunday in the Park with George,* and *Sweeney Todd.* On his last visit with Hammerstein before his death in 1960, Sondheim asked him to sign a portrait the older man had given him. The inscription read, "For Stevie, My Friend and Teacher." High praise from a mentor to a protégé, and emblematic of the generous spirit Hammerstein possessed.[73]

Joy as a Source of Energy

Joy is generative. It is something that feeds upon itself. We can smile at the simple pleasures of life—a baby gurgling, a toddler taking a first step, a school kid proudly showing off something she made at school. We laugh with colleagues in a funny situation at work or something silly that occurred on your way to work. There is joy in our laughter.

I often tell people I meet for the first time that I take my work seriously but not myself. The work that I do gives me pleasure. There is joy for me in writing, teaching, and coaching, as well as playing golf and practicing piano. And in my work, I find humor in everyday things. Jokes such as these can lighten up any situation:

- *I had planned to attend the meeting, but something came up. The socks in my drawers needed re-arranging.*

- *My performance review was so bad, my boss was actually crying. "Relax," I said, "You give me a raise and we'll both feel better."*

- *Turning sixty-five is like graduating from high school. It's an achievement that comes from putting in the time. But there is a positive. My Mom says I can stay out till midnight as long as I don't make any noise when I come home.*

- *When you get older, you get all kinds of senior discounts for things like restaurants and movies. Even cruises. I saw an ad for a senior cruise that showed bikini-clad women who looked to be in their early 20s . . . On the other hand, if my wife caught me with a woman so young, she would smile and tip the young lady $10 for walking me back to my room.*

Joy makes us feel good to be alive, if only for a moment. It also renews our sense of humanity. Yes, life can be difficult but with luck, there is still room for laughter. That is one reason oppressed people find humor. For millennia Jews were marginalized from Western society. As a result, the Jewish tradition is replete with situational humor that spits in the face of the oppressor. A similar kind of humor developed in the USSR with many jokes about the unfairness of the communist system. Soldiers in wartime also tell jokes. In those situations, it's an affirmation of self in a terrible predicament. A joke says yes, I am alive. *"Pain plus time equals humor" is* a "formula" that the late Garry Marshall, creator and producer of memorable sitcoms like *Happy Days, Laverne and Shirley* and *Mork and Mindy*, said he learned from observing comedian, Lenny Bruce.[74]

Humor emerging from pain is humankind's way of coping with hurt. Some people would turn that pain into rage; others turn it into a catalyst for self-improvement. Comedians turn that pain into gold. Humor is generative, and Humor is one way to deal with the challenges facing you. Find ways you can laugh at the world around you. And in the process feel better about what you do and with whom you work.

Laughter as Energy

One man who found hope and solace in humor was Abraham Lincoln. As successful as he became, his life was marked with tragedy including the death of his mother and the loss of his son, Todd. His wife Julia also suffered from bouts of depression, something that afflicted him too. As President, Lincoln presided over the bloodiest war in American history.

Humor was his safety valve. He liked nothing more than to entertain guests with stories about or from his days as a circuit-riding lawyer in Illinois. He loved to spin the yarns as well as hear new stories. Sometimes those around him would grow weary of his stories, to wit Lincoln once quipped, "Gentlemen, why don't you laugh? With the fearful strain that is upon me night and day, if I did not laugh I should die, and you need this medicine as much as I do." Part of the "medicine" Lincoln dispensed were stories told about himself and many at his own expense.

"I was once accosted," said Lincoln, "by a stranger, who said, 'Excuse me, sir, but I have an article in my possession which rightfully belongs to you.' 'How is that?' I asked, considerably astonished. The stranger took a jackknife from his pocket.

'This knife,' said he, 'was placed in my hands some years ago with the injunction that I was to keep it until I found a man uglier than myself. I have carried it from that time to this. Allow me now to say, sir, that I think you are fairly entitled to the property.'"75

Humor, as Lincoln used it, helped him navigate dark days. It can also lighten the mood. Norm Eisen, who served as ambassador to the Czech Republic in the mid-2000s, tells the story about one of his predecessors, Shirley Temple Black. Yes, that Shirley Temple—the 1930s child star. Ms. Black was serving in Prague when the communist dictatorship fell and so she gathered her team around her in a staff meeting. Then, as Eisen tells it, "She stood up, and said, 'I'm only going to do this once' and then broke into a rendition of the song, "The Good Ship Lollipop" as she danced around the table. Eisen says her staff—all of them "hardened cold warriors"— "broke into applause at the end because her fundamental optimism had proven correct."[76]

Novelist Charlotte Wood gave a speech on the power of laughter. In her speech, portions of which were reprinted in *The Guardian*, Wood describes laughter for an author as "a sense of lightness, of joy, the sense of possibility that comes when laughter enters a work of literature, whether it's manifest on the page itself or merely as part of the writer's process. For laughter is a sharp instrument, as it turns out, capable of performing many crucial, and I think profound, functions." Wood writes that "laughter is a very powerful tool of connection. It allows us to see that we are all human; we are all children; we all fail. There's a sense of shared relief immediately attended, I think, by a shared forgiveness."

For Wood, an Australian, laughter can be relief from pain, resistance to things beyond our control and as a creative force that is generative. Laughter, too, can be an instrument of truth. Laughter has that ability to deflate over-inflated egos, and in the process, reveal the pomposity within in. Finally, according to Wood, laughter is a call to optimism. It is a belief in a better possibility. Wood quotes her friend writer and critic, Tegan Bennett Daylight, who advises her writing students to "cultivate a sense of humor as they write," including themselves. Daylight says, "When we're laughing at ourselves, we're being honest about who we are—we're telling the truth."[77]

Closing thought

Grace, as we have discovered, is rooted in working for the "greater good." It demands acting with respect and compassion. It requires energy that like grace itself is generative. It renews itself through practice as well as by taking in life, doing one's best, enjoying the highlights, mourning the losses, and doing so in the full spirit of life.

In forgiveness, mercy, joy, and humor. Grace is ultimately our gift to ourselves. Our challenge is to use it wisely and use it often.

> **FINDING SOURCES OF ENERGY FROM WITHIN OURSELVES IS ESSENTIAL TO MAKING GRACE COME ALIVE IN OUR LIVES AND IN THE LIVES OF OTHERS.**

Energy: What the Leaders Say

Energy is the catalyst within us that engages our awareness and challenges us to do something.

***

"It's our capacity to get stuff done," says Christine Porath. "Our energy is the fuel of high performance. For people that achieve great results over a sustained period, they need to be enthusiastic about the effort they put into their work or any other effort. So, I think energy is really the fuel for that."

For Mike McKinney, "energy is more of a commitment to stay the course, to do the hard thing over and over, regardless of the context . . . you're reconnecting with your purpose. You're reconnecting with your values. And you're realigning those things with your behavior, with those values." And as a result, you end up energizing yourself.

"We all face adversity from time to time and it can suck the life out of you," says Mike McKinney. "I try to remember to do three things which are usually the first things to go when faced with a problem. First, get your sleep. We make bad decisions when we are tired. Second, keep your mind on the big picture. Whatever you are facing is part of your world, it's not your world. And finally, stay connected. It's easy to walk away. Stick around and be part of the solution."

"Energy, for me, is two different things —physical and mental," says Scott Moorehead. Physical energy requires appropriate care, feeding and exercise. "But I think the thing that tires out first in most people is mental energy. You can become mentally spent very quickly. There's only a certain amount of energy before things start to deteriorate and functions start to stop."

Scott has found ways to recharge by practicing meditation and mindfulness, but he does something else. When he is in need of a "re-charge," he closes the door to his office and has a board meeting with himself as he jokes but what he does next gets to the heart of the matter. "I will ask myself a very thought-provoking question, such as 'If our company could talk, what would it say right now?'" And then he thinks for a while and writes his thoughts into his journal.

Tim Sanders approaches energy in a similar fashion. That is, showing grace by slowing down, by breathing deeply and slowly. Doing so will enable you to be more in the moment and therefore enable yourself to act with a spirit of grace, that is, be cool, be calm, be rational and be present. "If you take the word slow, S-L-O-W, into your meeting you'll walk out showing grace." That's been my number one nugget of advice. You'll walk out showing grace."

Skip Prichard received an early introduction into the concept of energy. He recalls visiting an elderly relative in a nursing home and seeing a very old man seemingly drained of all energy. Yet when he was put near a piano, "you would see a complete transformation as soon as his fingers touched the keys. Within a minute, you wouldn't even recognize this man as the same person. Why is that? He tapped into his energy source deep within. And we all have this energy source inside us." Skip adds, "when you see someone's energy come, you sense a purity. And you sense something about them. And you want to know where it comes from, what they're about, and what their talents are."

Stephen M.R. Covey sees four kinds of energy—joy, passion, creative, and organizational. Each in its own way nurtures the sense of grace for giver and receiver. As Stephen says, "joy is the happiness and satisfaction. The fun. The energy is actual physical energy. It's energizing to be trusted. There is also "emotional energy. That's passion.

That's not the suffering passion but the excitement passion and such, to tap into someone's greatest sense of meaning and purpose." Thirdly there is creative energy that expresses itself as innovation, which is nurtured by a sense of trust. And finally, there is energy that comes from being around people, something Stephen calls "engagement, which commits people. We achieve greater commitment because of what that does to us."

Finally, energy emerges from inspiration. "Energy is inspiration. It's inspiring... That word, to *inspire*, energizes and means to breathe into. Energy comes from life and from breath. It's energizing. To me, inspiration is a product of that energy. I make the point on trust that to be trusted is the most inspiring form of human motivation. It brings out the best in all of us . . . extending and giving and receiving grace is also inspiring to all. When there's inspiration, there's energy."

Stephen goes on, "Giving of grace is also physically energizing," says Stephen. "I think it energizes a person to receive grace. And I think it energizes a person to give grace. To give generosity. To give respect. To give abundance. To give trust."

***

Think about these questions:

- How can you channel your energy into purposeful action?

- What specific steps will you keep up your energy levels?

- How can you share your energy with others so they feel they can deal with the challenges they face?

- How do you renew your energy?

- How can you rid yourself of "de-energizing" attacks?

- How do you become a better collaborator?

- How can you maximize joy in your life?

- How can we recharge ourselves through laughter?

Graceful Leadership Steps

Energy—*focusing your energy on making a positive difference*

- Find ways to recharge yourself so you can optimize your actions.

- Be mindful of yourself—what can you do to help yourself?

- Be mindful of others—what can you do to help others?

- Re-energize yourself by taking time off from work to pursue what you love to do.

- Set aside times of the day when you will "disconnect" from smart devices. Look at life around you, not what's on your screen.

- Spend time with family to re-connect to what is most important in your life.

- Make time to see friends and while with them, enjoy their company.

- Keep yourself physically fit: exercise regularly, eat wisely, and get enough sleep.

A Leader's Guide to a Better Us

Focus on Better

This book has focused on the many ways that grace touches our lives. Our challenge is to put its principles into practice. One way to begin is to adopt a mindset I will call "Focus on Better."

Make a difference in the lives of others. And that's why I like the idea of "better." We can do *better*.

Better for me means being a more supportive friend, relative or colleague. Being there without being asked. That is, where there is a need, pitch in without being asked. Do things to make people happier. That could be as simple as smiling more or offering to hold the door for someone.

Do so in a spirit of openness, not obligation.

You might define better as involvement. Pick your topic and put yourself into it. For example, look at your job. If you are deficient in an area, bone up on it, either through study or by asking others for help. In your community, look into areas of need, what could you do to make things better for just one person?

Adding steel to the spine of better, let's include the admonition: no whining. Whining depletes our energy. It draws us away from doing what we should be doing, not simply for others but for ourselves. Whining is the enemy of better.

Notably, we will fail many times, either at doing better or at something else, but if we focus on a positive like "better" we will be pointing ourselves in the right direction. [78]

Graceful Self-Assessment

Consider how you are practicing the principles of grace. Consider this self-assessment as a tool to help you improve, not a way to give yourself a pat on the back for how good you think you are.

Use a 5-point scale to rate your behaviors with 5 being best, 1 being worst.

As an individual . . .

____ I practice humility on a daily basis.

____ I recognize my limitations but do not use them as an excuse for not doing something.

____ I strive to look for the good in others before making a judgment about them.

____ I consider it my responsibility to do something for the "greater good."

____ I make sacrifices in my own personal comfort so that others can benefit.

____ I am generous with my time to people in need.

____ I forgive those who have wronged me before I ask them to apologize for their mistakes.

____ I use my energy to do one kind thing for someone every day.

____ I believe that compassion involves showing mercy on those who have been wronged.

____ I respect the dignity of others because it is what I am called upon to do.

____ **Sub-total**

As a leader . . .

____ I practice humility as a means of opening myself up to learning from others.

____ I behave as if I am "the smartest person in the room" because I know if I do others will stay silent.

____ I assume people who work with me are acting with the best intentions until they prove otherwise.

____ I act for the "greater good" of the team before acting on what's good for me.

____ I make time to listen to others even when it means I cannot focus on my immediate demands.

____ I make those with whom I converse feel wanted and empowered.

____ I insist that forgiveness be a team practice by allowing those who have transgressed the opportunity to make amends.

_____   I derive my energy from watching my colleagues succeed.

_____   I believe that compassion involves showing concern through positive actions, not simply nice words.

_____   I insist that our team practice dignity for others by showing respect for colleagues through their words and their actions.

_____   Sub-total

_____   Total Score

Note: I understand that my score is not a testament to how good I am but rather an assessment of how much more I can do.

***

GRACE: The Role Leaders Play

Each leader I interviewed answered the following question: *What's one thing each of us could do to make things better for others?*

***

"I almost always start with working together on connecting and practicing gratefulness . . . If you can practice gratefulness, you can remove a lot of roadblocks that stand between you and progress . . . Practicing gratefulness is an extremely simple but very powerful tactic."

—Scott Moorehead

"One of the complaints I hear most is that someone isn't paying attention or listening to me. Having empathy or showing compassion, a lot of it starts with paying attention or listening."

—Christine Porath

"Learn to listen well. We're in an era where you can think about these grand things and these grand plans to answer that question, but to me, it's the simple act of putting down your device and listening."

—Skip Prichard

"The one thing I think we could do to make things better for others—what I always try to practice—to ascribe good motives to people unless I really have evidence that they don't have others' interests at heart. People can say the wrong thing. People can be off in their presentation. But I find that looking, always making the presumption that they're doing this with good intentions is an important and helpful thing."

—Sally Helgesen

"Self-improvement comes down to reflecting about where I am and where I want to be and what steps I need then to take now to get me there. . ."

—Mike McKinney

"The three things that I think all of us want to continue to improve, develop from . . . as who we are, three words: humility, love, and service . . . And when it comes to the leadership point of view, it is in creating and nurturing this environment with the reliable working together principles, practices, and management system."

—Alan Mulally

"In the next interaction that you have, whether it's at home or work or on the street, when you engage in a conversation and listen for what the other person might need, see if you could provide it for them."

—Wayne Baker

"The simple thing from a humanity perspective is to smile genuinely and be intentional about being present everywhere I go."

—Dave Johnson

"Lead out in extending trust to others. Find the ways. The opportunities. Whether you call it extending trust or believing in someone. Seeing the good in someone. Taking a chance on someone. You might use other language that might resonate with different people in different ways. I frame it as leading out and extending trust to others."

—Stephen M.R. Covey

"Expand our intellectual resources so that we can give them away. Study. Expand your horizons everyday you're alive . . . I believe that the more knowledge you possess, the more likely you are to share it and the bigger difference you can make. And the easier it is for you to accept those occasional losses in life because they come."

—Tim Sanders

Greatness & Grace

Greatness is a desire to achieve. When focused through the prism of grace, greatness becomes the impetus for doing one's best on behalf of others.

***

"Greatness is love personified," says Alaina Love. "We see it in action by individuals demonstrating a degree of interest in the world, interest in others, a belief that whatever they're doing, the world is bigger than they are. They carry themselves with a sense of deep interconnectedness with others, even others that are very different or appear to be very different from themselves. They have a sense that they're here to do something that is contributory in the world. So, their focus isn't on [themselves]. Their focus is on how can I take my gifts and use those gifts to give to others, to give to the world in a larger sense?"

Scott Moorehead echoes this theme. "Greatness within the concept of doing good is to create deep connections and be inspiring." The challenge is to do it long-term. "And in order to do that, you truly need to create deep connections. And if you're inspiring, you're ultimately allowing others the motivation to personally get involved in doing good as well."

Likewise, Skip Prichard believes, "Greatness is not only showing up and performing at an exceptional level but inspiring everyone around you to reach deep inside and reach their potential . . . It's not just my individual performance, but I'm the catalyst to make everybody show up with their individual strengths. And then you have greatness . . . You want to be that catalyst. And to be that catalyst, you have to be fully [engaged]."

"The path to greatness is all about service," says Mike McKinney. "Greatness means putting more of an emphasis on duty and less on personal desire. It gets back to that whole concept of sacrifice for others . . . Our greatness comes from sharing who we are with as many people as we can." Integral to greatness within the context of grace is sacrifice, which Mike defines as "doing what's best for others" ahead of self-interest. Sacrifice then becomes a kind of skin in the game with the person you are seeking to help.

Love & Grace

Love is a manifestation of compassion.

***

Chris Lowney says, love becomes "what's good" for the other rather than the self. It's a wish for happiness as well a desire for talent development. Love expresses itself as this thought: "I want you to flourish as a human being." Chris cites the quotation from Thomas Aquinas, "To love is to will the good of another."

For Alaina Love, the concept of love is "interconnectedness." It is "an accepting of the interconnectedness that we share with other people and a desire to create an environment where everybody is thriving."

Tim Sanders believes that "when you possess love for someone, grace is a bias. Just like when people love you, they presume you're good until proven bad at everything you do. I believe that love creates a lot of possibilities and one of them is a graceful outlook just like a gracious outlook. Think about that word, gracious."

Forgiveness & Grace

Forgiveness is an attribute of grace that enables us to look at those who have wronged us and move past the hurt. It is also something we must do for ourselves when we do wrong.

***

Sally Helgsen says, "To forgive or show mercy is by definition magnanimous. Grace is magnanimous because it connects us with goodness in the world."

Alaina Love has thought long and hard about what it means to forgive. "Forgiveness requires the release of anger and blame, which is difficult if you believe that you've somehow been slighted."

Alaina also integrates the concept of mercy. "Offering mercy requires that you recognize that your true power comes through forgiveness, not the positional power that allows you to punish. When truly inhabiting Grace, a leader is able to look past the slights of others, show mercy as easily as they mete out punishment, and will work to learn from the experience, or support the other person in learning from it. Balancing forgiveness and mercy with accountability is a real test of leadership and character, a test of Grace."

"Saying I forgive, but I don't forget,' notes Tim Sanders, is "like saying this is a 'new and improved" version of forgiveness. You can't possibly do both at the same time." Forgiveness is both transactional and transformational. The act of forgiveness is a transaction that affects the receiver. Moreover, that act is transformational for the giver because he or she is "wiping the slate clean" and moving forward. For Tim, "Forgiveness is like wiping the whiteboard clean. That's why it is such a wonderful gift when the other person receives forgiveness, true forgiveness . . . it transforms the giver more than the taker."

Civility & Grace

Civility lays the foundation for positive dialogue. When people look at others as human beings rather than as opponents, you can begin to have a conversation.

***

Civility is essential to organizational norms but as Mike explains it's more than being polite. "It's important to remember civility and grace, down to controlling our desires and inclinations for the sake of others, even sacrificing our rights to uphold the dignity of another person." Mike pins the blame for incivility on those in charge: "where we see bad behavior, there's been bad leadership."

Mike McKinney has been a business owner for decades. "Leadership to me starts with a commitment to people," says Mike. The leader adds value but his or her bigger role is to bring out the best in others. The challenge "means acting in the interests, the best interests of others, giving them exposure and putting them in the way of opportunities."

Graceful Guide to Leading with Grace

A fundamental tenet of leadership is responsibility for others. Leaders provide direction and then help people arrive at the destination. As such leaders must exemplify behaviors that encourage followership. Chief among them is setting the right example, that is, "leading with grace." Here are some suggestions.

- Share the Vision. Communicate the purpose of your organization, the why, and what you and your people do.

- Work the Mission. Exemplify what it means to do the work by keeping yourself in the loop about what's happening.

- Live the Values. Be the first to set the example by holding yourself accountable for living the values of your culture.

- Reflect on what you do and why regularly. Engage in conversations with trusted colleagues about important issues.

- Invite feedback from those who report to you. Make it safe for them to give you the "straight talk."

- Maintain composure when things get hot. Lowering your voice demonstrates self-control.

- Avoid zero-sum "victories." We win, you lose is a recipe for division. Leaders must unite, not divide.

- Seek comity. Make it known that you expect people to cooperate and collaborate with each other.

- Strive for patience. Learn to listen before you speak. Encourage the same behavior in others.

- Celebrate diversity. Make inclusion of different points of view a hallmark of your leadership.

- Enjoy what you do. Strive to bring a positive attitude to the workplace.

Graceful Guide to Mentoring

Mentoring is an investment in the development of another individual, typically a person just beginning his or her career. The mentor serves as a kind of wise old uncle (or aunt) whose only motive is to help the younger person succeed. Mentorship succeeds when the mentor is available, that is, serve as a trusted resource for guidance about work-life issues as well as career decisions. Mentorship, like grace, is given freely and without strings attached.

Here are some suggestions for establishing guidelines for successful mentorship:

- Be available. Mentors are selected because they have rich experience and success in their careers. They are willing to share what they have learned as a means of helping a younger colleague succeed.

- Share your expertise in ways that invite questions, not create a roadmap. That is, a mentor advises, not demands.

- Employ coaching techniques, when required. That is, you can help the mentee learn in three ways:

  - one, listen to what they say (or don't say);

  - two, ask open-ended questions to provoke greater understanding; and

  - three, be sparing with advice, e.g. better to have the mentee discover for him/herself.

- Observe the mentee over time to see how he or she grows and develops.

- Be ready to step back and away when the mentoring process is over. Good mentors let their proteges fly on their own. They are available when needed but understand that less of them is better for the mentee's future.

Every mentoring relationship will be different because the needs and wants of individuals vary from person to person. Mentors must be flexible at the same time they are entitled to limit their participation, especially if the mentee requires advise in areas where the mentor is not expert.

Graceful Guide to Optimism

Optimism is essential to the human condition. Learning ways to nurture and develop positive emotions are essential to sound mental health and can also improve physical health, too. Listed are eight skills developed by Dr. Judith Moskowitz at Northwestern University's Feinberg School of Medicine. Dr. Moskowitz says that if you practice three per day, you will find your mood has improved.[79]

- Recognize a positive event each day.

- Savor that event and log it in a journal or tell someone about it.

- Start a daily gratitude journal.

- List a personal strength and note how you used it.

- Set an attainable goal and note your progress.

- Report a relatively minor stress and list ways to reappraise the event positively.

- Recognize and practice small acts of kindness daily.

- Practice mindfulness, focusing on the here and now, rather than on the past or future.

Using Grace to Deliver Service to Others

Adopting a Service Ethos

Grace calls us to reach out to help others, that is, to find ways to serve them. Consider how you can adopt a mindset that enables you do think of how you can serve your colleagues by doing what you do and feel better about it?

Consider how you might:

- Listen, not judge *(keep an open mind)*

- Replace "have to" with "want to" *(when it comes to doing your work)*

- Put benefits ahead of activity *(how does this help others?)*

- Adopt a me-last attitude *(be humble)*

- Step out of the limelight *(share credit; take blame)*

Would these ideas work for you? If so, why? If not, why not?

What else might you to do to serve your colleagues and thereby serve your team and yourself?

Defining Grace through Service

An act of service toward a colleague can be anything of value you to do assist a colleague do his/her job better. In taking such action, you help that individual become a better contributor and collaborator. Such service can be:

- An intended act of kindness

- A pat on the back

- Help with "heavy lifting"

- Cheerful as well as effective

Or just do whatever you can do to make a situation better for someone else.

Creating a Service Ethos

Responsibility for creating a great place to work is a leader's job. But not solely! Employees have a role to play. Effective organization works more smoothly when colleagues cooperate and collaborate. This can only happen when employees view their colleagues as people they want to help out. In order to facilitate stronger levels of cooperation, it is useful to think of the employee as a "friend," someone you want to see succeed.

To make that happen you need to understand how you and your colleagues fit into the organization. The following questions will help.

- **What is my role?** Knowing what you do as well as what you are expected to do is critical to understanding your role in the company.

- **What is my colleague's role?** Knowing what others do is equally important because if you don't understand their role, you cannot assist them.

- **What can I do to help?** Consider actions steps you can take. They may be as simple as being timely or courteous. This may be as time-consuming as actually helping them complete a task.

- **What's stopping you from helping out?** Some people resist help. None of us like meddlers. Being "of service" is not interfering; it's offering assistance.

- **How do you know when you are succeeding?** Serving others works when it facilitates work. People work more efficiently and more cooperatively. Morale is better when people enjoy what they do and the people they work with.

Answers to these questions provide a foundation for taking the first step toward facilitating better working relations with colleagues. What you do is up to you.

Acknowledgements

The idea of me writing about grace may strike those who know me as odd. There is little about me that others may discern as graceful. It's more like I'm clumsy and awkward at times, both in speech and on the golf course. Yet I do know I have been touched by grace because I am blessed with family, friends and colleagues who serve as my role models. This book represents my attempt to discuss at length why grace is important and what it means to us now.

To pull this off I needed the assistance of many, beginning with the many folks I interviewed on the topic of grace. They are Wayne Baker, Louis Carter, Stephen M.R. Covey, Sally Helgesen, Dave Johnson, Alaina Love, Chris Lowney, Mike McKinney, Scott Moorehead, Alan Mulally, Christine Porath, Skip Prichard and Tim Sanders. I am grateful to each for time spent with me, and more importantly, the great insights they so readily shared with me. I thank them for their generosity.

I am deeply grateful to Dan Vega and the team at Indigo River Publishing—Bobby Dunaway who got this book into shape and my editor Deborah DeNicola,. Lucky for me, Deborah is not only an author, she also teaches English composition and grammar to college students.

I want to extend a hand to my fellow "book club" members—Jerry, Dan, Stew, Jim and Rob (plus Tom)—who readily share their views about all things meaningful, including a few things that are less significant—golf, college sports, and stupid things that men of a certain age still find funny.

164 · JOHN BALDONI

And of course, I thank my wife, Gail Campanella, who not only puts up with me, but whose patience I need and whose insights I cherish. Her careful reading and incisive edits have made this book better than I could have made it myself.

ENDNOTES

Prologue

1. David Brooks "Anthony Kennedy and the Privatization of Meaning" *New York Times* 6/29/2018 https://www.nytimes.com/2018/06/28/opinion/anthony-kennedy-individualism.html

2. Gregory Boyle Barking to the Choir: The *Power of Radical Kinship* New York: Simon & Schuster 2017 p. 10

Chapter 1: Why Grace

3. "Obituary: Aretha Franklin died on August 16, 2018" *The Economist 8/23/2108* https://www.economist.com/obituary/2018/08/23/aretha-franklin-died-on-august-16th

Jon Pareles "Aretha Franklin, Indomitable 'Queen of Soul,' Dies at 76" New York Times 8/16/2018 https://www.nytimes.com/2018/08/16/obituaries/aretha-franklin-dead.html

"100 Greatest Singers of All Time" Rolling Stone magazine 12/03/2010 https://www.rollingstone.com/music/music-lists/100-greatest-singers-of-all-time-147019/aretha-franklin-6-227696/

Gabrielle Horn (article) Interview by Cynthia Canty "The Queen of Soul pursued her love of opera until the very end" *Stateside* Michigan Radio 8/16/2018 http://www.michiganradio.org/post/queen-soul-pursued-her-love-opera-until-very-end

Gary Graff "15 Best Performances During Aretha Franklin's Funeral, a Celebration Fit for a Queen" www.billboard.com 8/31/2018 https://www.billboard.com/articles/news/8473216/aretha-franklin-funeral-best-performances-list

Clarissa Hamlin "From Al Sharpton to Barack Obama: Here's How Aretha Franklin Was Celebrated At Her Funeral" Newsone 8/31/2018 https://newsone.com/3824528/aretha-franklin-funeral-quotes-eulogy/

Tomas Mier "Bill Clinton Jokes About Aretha Franklin's Multiple Casket Wardrobe Changes During Funeral Speech" People.com 8/31/2018 https://people.com/music/aretha-franklin-funeral-bill-clinton-tribute-wardrobe-change-jokes/

4. Kaufman Kohler, M.M. Eichler "Grace, Divine" http://www.jewishencyclopedia.com/articles/6842-grace-divine

Jeff A. Benner "Meaning of Grace from a Hebrew Tradition" http://www.ancient-hebrew.org/articles_grace.html

5. J. Hashmi "Grace, Faith and Works" (Part 1 of 4): The Components of Faith 2008 https://www.islamreligion.com/articles/1165/grace-faith-and-works-part-1/

6. "A Blessed Life" is a joint project of Donald Altman and Spirituality & Practice. E-Course Content copyright 2018 by Donald Altman.

7. John Baldoni "Babies R Us: Failing Store, Rising Grace" Forbes.com 5/02/2018 https://www.forbes.com/sites/johnbaldoni/2018/05/02/babies-r-us-failing-store-rising-grace/

Mackenzie Lewis Kassab "The Real American Job Crisis Isn't in the Coal Mines. It's at the Mall." *Glamour* 12/21/2017
https://www.glamour.com/gallery/the-real-american-job-crisis-is-in-retail

Dominic Rushie "The U.S. retail market is hemorrhaging jobs – and it's hitting women hardest" The *Guardian* 1/13/2018
https://www.theguardian.com/business/2018/jan/13/us-retail-sector-job-losses-hitting-women-hardest-data

8. John Baldoni "James Blake and creating grace" SmartBrief.com" 5/04/2018
http://www.smartbrief.com/original/2018/05/james-blake-and-creating-grace

Benjamin Mueller "New York City and James Blake Resolve Excessive-Force Claim" *New York Times* 6/20/2017

James Blake and Carol Taylor *Ways of Grace: Stories of Activism, Adversity, and How Sports Can Bring Us Together* New York: Amistad 2017

Arthur Ashe and Arnold Rampersad *Days of Grace: A Memoir* New York: Ballantine Books 1994

9. Scott Pelley "Prodigy Says She'd Prefer to Be the First Alma Over the Second Mozart" 60 Minutes CBS News 11/02/2017
https://www.cbsnews.com/news/12-year-old-prodigy-could-be-as-gifted-as-mozart/

Alma Deutscher https://en.wikipedia.org/wiki/Alma_Deutscher

Alma Deutscher website https://www.almadeutscher.com

Ben Lawrence "What Does an Opera by an Eleven-Year Old Sound Like?" *Daily Telegraph* 30 December 2016
https://www.telegraph.co.uk/opera/what-to-see/does-opera-11-year-old-sound-like/

"Alma Deutscher, composer – Violinist and Pianist – The World Around Us". *YouTube.com*. Zeitgeist Minds. Retrieved 27 November 2015.
https://www.youtube.com/watch?v=T3YlcHyF9dc

James Sohre "New Cinderella SRO in San Jose" *Opera Today*, 22 December 2017)
http://www.operatoday.com/content/2017/12/new_cinderella_.php

Dr. Wilhelm Sinkovicz, *Die Presse* 24 April 2018 reprised at https://www.facebook.com/AlmaDeutscher/posts/a-wonderful.../806627379541412/

Nicholas Wroe "Alma Deutscher: the 10-year-old who is making the music world listen" The Guardian 05 February 2016
https://www.theguardian.com/music/2016/feb/05/alma-deutscher-10-music-world

"ORF report about Cinderella". YouTube.com. Retrieved 31 December 2016.
https://youtu.be/wxgRGAVSKXs

Elizabeth Grice "An opera at seven, a concerto at nine: meet Britain's reluctant heir to Mozart" *The Daily Telegraph*. 25 June 2016 [Little Alma]

10. Walter Isaacson *Leonardo DaVinci* New York: Simon & Schuster Paperbacks 2017 p 31. [Citing Anthony Grafton *Leon Battista Alberti: Master Architect of the Italian Renaissance* Cambridge MA: Harvard Press 2002; see also Franco Borsi *Leon Battista Alberti* New York: Harper & Row, 1975]

11. James Martin, S.J. "The grace filled encounter between Paul McCartney and James Corden" America Magazine 6/26/2018 https://www.americamagazine.org/faith/2018/06/26/grace-filled-encounter-between-paul-mccartney-and-james-corden

Chapter 2: Generosity

12. Tom Junod "Can You Say… Hero?" *Esquire* 5/06/2017 originally published in November 1998 issue of *Esquire* magazine
https://www.esquire.com/entertainment/tv/a27134/can-you-say-hero-esq1198/

Won't You Be My Neighbor? Director: Morgan Neville; Tremolo Productions 2018

David Brooks "Fred Rogers and the Loveliness of the Little Good" *New York Times* 7/5/2018 [Citing the story of the boy with cerebral palsy]

13. David Maraniss *When Pride Still Mattered: A Life of Vince Lombardi* (New York: Simon & Schuster 1999) pp. 405-6

14. John Baldoni *Great Motivation Secrets of Great Leaders* New York: (McGraw Hill, 2005) pp. 40-41; David H. Hackworth and Eilhys England *Steel My Soldiers' Hearts* (New York: Rugged Land) p. 94 (Quote)

15. Jason Kurtz "LeBron: Trump is using sports to divide us" CNN.com 7/31/2018 [Interview with Don Lemon]
https://www.cnn.com/2018/07/30/politics/lebron-james-trump-akron-school-lemon-cnntv/index.html

16. Rachel Martin "Principal of LeBron James' I Promise School Talks About Mission" Morning Edition NPR 8/1/2018
https://www.npr.org/2018/08/01/634492350/principal-of-lebron-james-i-promise-school-talks-about-mission

I Promise Mission
http://www.lebronjamesfamilyfoundation.org/page/wheelsforeducation#wfePromise

Tania Ganguli "LeBron James has one more career-defining moment in his home state, opening a public school in Akron" *Los Angeles Times* 7/30/2018
http://www.latimes.com/sports/lakers/la-sp-lakers-lebron-james-i-promise-20180729-htmlstory.html
http://www.latimes.com/sports/lakers/la-sp-lakers-lebron-james-i-promise-20180729-htmlstory.html

17. John Baldoni "Mentors Matter One Person at a Time" *Forbes.com* 6/01/2016
https://www.forbes.com/sites/johnbaldoni/2016/06/01/mentors-matter-one-person-at-a-time/

18. John Baldoni "How Mentors Can Help Mentors Succeed" *LinkedIn* 5/02/2018
https://www.linkedin.com/pulse/how-mentors-can-help-millennials-suc-ceed-john-baldoni/

Amy Adkins "What Millennials Want from Work and Life" Gallup.com 5/10/2016
https://www.gallup.com/workplace/236477/millennials-work-life.aspx

Jennifer F. Waljee M.D., Vineet Chopra, M.D. and Sanjay Saint "Mentoring Millennials" *JAMA Network* 4/17/2018

19. *The Man Who Knew Infinity* Written and directed by Matthew Brown 2015

Judd Apatow "The Zen Diaries of Garry Shandling" HBO 3/26/2108
https://www.hbo.com/documentaries/the-zen-diaries-of-garry-shandling

Robert Lloyd "Garry Shandling and Judd Apatow" *Los Angeles Times* 3/25/2018
http://www.latimes.com/entertainment/tv/la-et-st-garry-shandling-doc-judd-apatow-20180325-htmlstory.html

David Greene "Judd Apatow mines the mystery of his mentor: Garry Shandling" *Morning Edition* NPR 3/26/2018 https://www.npr.org/2018/03/26/596499818/judd-apatow-mines-the-mystery-of-his-mentor-garry-shandling

Matthew Seitz "*The Zen Diaries of Garry Shandling* Is an Intimate Portrait of a Comedy Pioneer" *Vulture.com* 3/26/2018 http://www.vulture.com/2018/03/the-zen-diaries-of-garry-shandling-hbo-review.html

20. John Baldoni "What a Golf Pro Taught Me Can Make You a Better Leader" Forbes.com 7/08/2105 https://www.forbes.com/sites/johnbaldoni/2015/07/08/what-a-golf-pro-taught-me-can-make-you-a-better-leader/

21. Diana Goetsch "Teaching William Zinsser to Write Poetry *The New Yorker* 3/06/2018 https://www.newyorker.com/culture/personal-history/teaching-william-zinsser-to-write-poetry

John Baldoni "How Good Managers Teach" SmartBrief.com 3/01/2019 https://www.smartbrief.com/original/2019/03/how-good-managers-teach

22. John Baldoni "Reciprocity Ring: When Giving at Work Becomes an Action Not a Check" Forbes.com 3/29/2018 https://www.forbes.com/sites/johnbaldoni/2018/03/29/the-reciprocity-ring-when-giving-at-work-becomes-an-act-not-a-check/

Jon Simons "Corporate Volunteerism: Paid-Time Off, Win Win" Monster.com [no date]

Giving in Numbers http://cecp.co/home/resources/giving-in-numbers/ 2017

Stine Rendrup Johansen "Study: Altruism is in our Genes" *Science Nordic* 8/30/2015 http://sciencenordic.com/study-altruism-our-genes

Author interview with Wayne Baker on 8/10/2018

Kula Ring https://en.wikipedia.org/wiki/Kula_ring

Adam Grant "Adam Grant Can Help You Coax Generosity Out of Your Grumpiest Co-Workers" FastCompany.com 3/20/2018 https://www.fastcompany.com/40545869/adam-grant-can-help-you-coax-generosity-out-of-your-grumpiest-coworker

Background material on the Reciprocity Ring and Givitas was sourced at https://www.giveandtakeinc.com/

Note: the terms "respectful engagement" and "task enablement" come from the research work of Jane Dutton, a professor of organizational development at the Ross School of Business at the University of Michigan.

23. Marcelo Cerullo MPH and Pamela Lipsett MD "Assessing the Magnitude of a Surgical Career Through His Trainees: The John L. Cameron Legacy Factor" Annals of Surgery May 2017 Volume 265-Issue 5 – pp. 866-868 https://journals.lww.com/annalsofsurgery/Fulltext/2017/05000/Assessing_the_Magnitude_of_a_Surgical_Career.5.aspx

Marcus Buckingham and Curt Coffman *First Break All the Rules: What the World's Best Managers Do Differently* New York: Simon & Schuster 1999

Chapter 3: Respect

24. John Baldoni "Gordie Howe: A Life Well Remembered" *Forbes.com* 6/15/2106
https://www.forbes.com/sites/johnbaldoni/2016/06/15/gordie-howe-a-life-well-re-membered/

Helene St. James "Touching Gordie Howe Eulogy Chuck Full of Anecdotes" *Detroit Free Press* 6/15/2016
https://www.freep.com/story/sports/nhl/red-wings/2016/06/15/gordie-howe-funeral/85926292/

Mark Snyder "Wayne Gretzky: Gordie Howe was the greatest player, nicest man I ever met" *Detroit Free Press* 6/14/2016
https://www.freep.com/story/sports/nhl/red-wings/2016/06/14/wayne-gretzky-gordie-howe/85862142/

Obituary: Muhammad Ali *The Economist* 6/11/2016
https://www.economist.com/obituary/2016/06/11/obituary-muhammad-ali

25. John Baldoni "Homeboy Humility: Growing Stronger and Better By Listening" Forbes.com 12/21/2017
https://www.forbes.com/sites/johnbaldoni/2017/12/21/homeboy-humility-growing-stronger-and-better-by-listening/

John Baldoni "Lessons from Father Greg Boyle: Eating Your Humble Pie" SmartBrief.com 8/24/2018
http://www.smartbrief.com/original/2018/08/lessons-father-greg-boyle-eating-your-humble-pie

Terry Gross "Priest Responds to Gang Members' 'Lethal Lack of Hope' with Jobs and Love" *Fresh Air* NPR 11/13/2017
https://www.npr.org/2017/11/13/563734736/priest-responds-to-gang-members-lethal-absence-of-hope-with-jobs-and-love

26. All quotes by Jimmy Carter were taken from a quotes page on Goodreads. https://www.goodreads.com/author/quotes/6113.Jimmy_Carter

Kevin Sullivan and Mary Jordan "The Un-Celebrity President" *Washington Post* 8/17/2018
https://www.washingtonpost.com/news/national/wp/2018/08/17/feature/the-un-celebrity-president-jimmy-carter-shuns-riches-lives-modestly-in-his-georgia-hometown

Remembering the Failed Iranian Mission April 25, 1980
http://arlingtoncemetery.net/iran-mission.htm

Steve Vogel "Remembering the Failed Iranian Mission" *Washington Post* 4/05/2000
https://www.washingtonpost.com/archive/local/2000/05/04/remembering-failed-iranian-mission/21c38ada-30f6-493f-9eb0-83549a0408d7/?utm_term=.8997ca660535

27. Interview with Alan Mulally 7/23/2108

28. John Baldoni "Chaplain Life Lessons" SmartBrief.com

Kerry Egan On Living City: Riverhead Books 2016

Terry Gross "Hospice Chaplain Reflects On Life, Death and the 'Strength of the Human Soul'" *Fresh Air* NPR 10/31/2016
https://www.npr.org/templates/transcript/transcript.php?storyId=499762656

29. Anderson Cooper "Feeding Puerto Rico" CBS 60 *Minutes* 11/26/2-17
https://www.cbsnews.com/news/feeding-puerto-rico/

Tim Carman "José Andrés's riveting 'We Fed an Island' calls for a revolution in disaster relief" *Washington Post* 9/06/2018 [Review of José Andrés and Richard Wolffe *We Fed an* Island New York: Anthony Bourdain/Ecco 2018
https://www.washingtonpost.com/lifestyle/food/jose-andress-riveting-we-fed-an-island-calls-for-a-revolution-in-disaster-relief/2018/09/05/b126d766-ad70-11e8-b1da-ff7faa680710_story.html

Anna Mazarakis "José Andrés came to the US with just $50 in his pocket and here's how he became a celebrity chef with 26 restaurants and 2 Michelin stars" *Business Insider* 10/07/2017
https://www.businessinsider.com/celebrity-chef-jose-andres-success-podcast-interview-2017-10

30. Terry Gross "As Marriage standards change, a therapist recommends rethinking fidelity" *Fresh Air* NPR 12/13/2017
https://www.npr.org/2017/12/13/570131890/as-marriage-standards-change-a-therapist-recommends-rethinking-infidelity

Esther Perel *The State of Affairs: Rethinking Fidelity* New York: Harper 2017

"The Decision That Transformed Tony Robbins' Life Forever." *Goalcast*, www.goalcast.com/2017/04/16/the-decision-that-transformed-tony-robbins-life-forever/.

31. John Baldoni "Hit 'em Straight: Nice Guys Know How to Play the Game" Forbes.com 7/21/2017

"Good Guys Award" 2017 *Golf Digest*
https://www.forbes.com/sites/johnbaldoni/2017/07/21/hit-em-straight-nice-guys-know-how-to-play-the-game/

John Baldoni "Jordan Spieth Gives a Lesson in Character Forbes.com 4/11/2016
https://www.forbes.com/sites/johnbaldoni/2016/04/11/jordan-speith-gives-a-lesson-in-character/

32. Author interview with Louis Carter conducted 8/08/2018

Most Love Workplace www.mostlovedworkplace.com

Best Practice Institute www.bestpracticesinstitute.org

Alisa Cohn "The Best Practices Institute Thinks Workplaces Should Be 'Emotionally Connected'" *Forbes.com* 4/09/2018
https://www.forbes.com/sites/alisacohn/2018/04/09/the-best-practice-institute-thinks-workplaces-should-be-emotionally-connected

33. "Michigan Radio's Mark Brush 'took care of everyone.' Now we say thank you and goodbye." Michigan Radio 3/23/2108
http://www.michiganradio.org/post/michigan-radio-s-mark-brush-took-care-everyone-now-we-say-thank-you-and-goodbye

Nomination letter to Committee for the MAPB Public Media Impact award written by Stephen Schram

Chapter 4: Action

34. Sophie Sherry "Flint Pediatrician helped expose water crisis. Now, she shares her story in new memoir." *Stateside* Michigan Radio 6/26/2018
http://michiganradio.org/post/flint-pediatrician-helped-expose-water-crisis-now-she-shares-her-story-new-memoir

Mona Hanna-Attisha *What The Eyes Don't See: A Story of Crisis, Resistance, and Hope in an American City* (New York: One World) 2018

Terry Gross "Pediatrician Who Exposed Flint Water Crisis Shares Her 'Story Of Resistance'" NPR *Fresh Air* 6/25/2018 [Bridget Bentz, Molly Seavy-Nesper and Scott Hensley adapted interview for the web.]
https://www.npr.org/sections/health-shots/2018/06/25/623126968/pediatri-cian-who-exposed-flint-water-crisis-shares-her-story-of-resistance

35. John Baldoni "Leaders Don't Make Deals about Ethics" *Forbes.com* 12/08/2017
https://www.forbes.com/sites/johnbaldoni/2017/12/08/leaders-dont-make-deals-about-ethics

McKay Coppins "The Vanishing Values Voter" *The Atlantic* 12/07/2107
https://www.theatlantic.com/politics/archive/2017/12/the-vanishing-values-vot-er/547772/

36. John Baldoni "How to Deliver Moral Leadership at Work" *Forbes.com* 4/12/2018
https://www.forbes.com/sites/johnbaldoni/2018/04/12/how-to-deliver-moral-leader-ship-to-employees/

"Report Employees Say Their Companies Would Perform Better If Their Leaders Showed 'Better More Leadership,'" New Study Says" LRN.com
http://lrn.com/news-archive/moral-leadership-report/

37. George Washington's *Rules of Civility & Decent Behavior in Company and Conversa-tion* Foundations Magazine [web only, not in print]
http://www.foundationsmag.com/civility.html

38. "Presiding Over the Congress: The Indispensable Man"
https://www.mountvernon.org/george-washington/constitutional-convention/conven-tion-president/

39. "Civility in America 2018: Civility at Work and in Our Public Squares" Report by Weber Shandwick, Powell Take and KRC Research
https://www.webershandwick.com/wp-content/uploads/2018/06/Civility-in-Ameri-ca-VII-FINAL.pdf

40. Gerard F. Seib "What Duluth can teach America about declining political civility" *Wall Street Journal* 7/30/2018
https://www.wsj.com/articles/what-duluth-can-teach-america-about-declining-politi-cal-civility-1532961081
http://dsaspeakyourpeace.org/about.html?mod=article_inline

P. M. Forni *Choosing Civility: The 25 Rules of Considerate Conduct* (New York: St. Mar-tin's Press) 2002

41. Lincoln Caplan "Our Towns: James and Deborah Fallows explore 'what the hell is happening in America'" *Harvard Magazine* May-June 2018
https://harvardmagazine.com/2018/05/our-towns-fallows

James Fallows and Deborah Fallows *Our Towns: 100,000 Mile Journey Into the Heart of America* (New York Penguin Random House) 2018

James Fallows "Eleven Signs a City Will Succeed" *The Atlantic* March 2016
https://www.theatlantic.com/magazine/archive/2016/03/eleven-signs-a-city-will-suc-ceed/426885/

42. David Brooks "Where American Renewal Begins" New York Times 7/26/2018
https://www.nytimes.com/2018/07/26/opinion/thread-baltimore-american-renew-al-community-program.html

43. David Brooks "A Really Good Thing Is Happening in America" *New York Times* 10.08/2018
https://www.nytimes.com/2018/10/08/opinion/collective-impact-community-civic-architecture.html

44. John Baldoni "After Pittsburgh, Words of Strength in the Face of Hate." *SmartBrief.* October 31, 2018.
https://www.smartbrief.com/original/2018/10/after-pittsburgh-words-strength-face-hate.

45. John Baldoni "Remembering Brent Taylor: Mayor, Major And Man Of Service" Forbes.com 11/06/2018
https://www.forbes.com/sites/johnbaldoni/2018/11/06/remembering-brent-taylor-mayor-major-and-man-of-service/

"Major Taylor's Widow Speaks Publicly For First Time Since Husband's Death" *KSL5-TV.com* 11/06/2018
https://ksltv.com/402937/brent-taylor/

Rachel Martin "Utah Town Honors Its Mayor, A National Guardsman, Who Was Killed In Kabul NPR *Morning Edition* 11/02/2108
https://www.npr.org/2018/11/06/664617069/utah-town-honors-its-mayor-a-national-guardsman-who-was-killed-in-kabul

Amy B. Wang "'I have given my life to serve': Utah mayor and father of seven killed in Afghanistan" *Washington Post* 11/04/2108
https://www.washingtonpost.com/national-security/2018/11/04/i-have-given-my-life-serve-utah-mayor-father-seven-killed-afghanistan/

46. John Baldoni "Management: Good Service Begins (and Ends) with Good Values" Forbes.com 5/07/2014
https://www.forbes.com/sites/johnbaldoni/2014/05/07/management-good-service-begins-and-ends-with-good-values/

47. Jonathan Lapook "Aly Raisman Speaks Out about Sexual Abuse" CBS 60 Minutes 9/09/2018
https://www.cbsnews.com/news/aly-raisman-60-minutes-us-olympic-gold-medal-gymnast-i-am-a-victim-of-sexual-abuse/

48. John Baldoni "When Tragedy Strikes" Smartbrief.com 10/5/2018
https://www.smartbrief.com/original/2018/10/when-tragedy-strikes

We Were Not Found Wanting *Letters of Note* August 9, 2011
http://www.lettersofnote.com/2011/08/we-were-not-found-wanting.html

Wikipedia: Parkland (film) https://en.wikipedia.org/wiki/Parkland_(film)

Vincent Bugliosi *Reclaiming History: The Assassination of President John F. Kennedy* New York: W.W. Norton 2007

49. Carlos Monarrez "Jim Brandstatter on Lions/WJR ouster: 'We all got blindsided'" Detroit Free Press 7/10/2108
https://www.freep.com/story/sports/nfl/lions/2018/07/10/jim-brandstatter-detroit-lions-wjr-ouster/772554002/

Angelique S. Chengelis and James David Dixon "Lions Brandstatter 'blindsided by firing at broadcast' Detroit News 7/10/2017
https://www.detroitnews.com/story/news/local/michigan/2018/07/10/jim-brandstatter-let-go-wjr-760/771249002/

Carlos Monarrez "Ex-Lions voice Brandstatter deserved better than this" *Detroit Free Press* 7/13/201
https://www.freep.com/story/sports/nfl/lions/2018/07/13/detroit-lions-jim-brandstatter-fired/782276002/

Kirkland Crawford "Detroit Lions radio: Jim Brandstatter 'passes the torch to Lomas Brown" Detroit Free Press 7/14/2018
https://www.freep.com/story/sports/nfl/lions/2018/07/14/detroit-lions-jim-brandstatter-lomas-brown/785389002/

50. Transcript of John McCain's Concession Speech 11/5/2008
https://www.npr.org/templates/story/story.php?storyId=96631784 Produced and directed by Peter Kunhardt and Teddy Kunhardt

John McCain: For Whom the Bell Tolls HBO 5/28/2018
https://www.hbo.com/documentaries/john-mccain-for-whom-the-bell-tolls

Bret Stephens "Straining to Keep Faith With America" *New York Times* 8/31/2018
https://www.nytimes.com/2018/08/31/opinion/mccain-america.html [Citing excerpt from John McCain with Mark Salter *Faith of My Fathers* New York: Random House 1999] Kayla Epstein "5 of John McCain's Most Courageous Political Moments" *Washington Post* 7/24/2107 [Arab comment] https://www.washingtonpost.com/news/the-fix/wp/2017/07/20/five-of-john-mccains- most-courageous-political-moments

Jake Tapper "Comments from Senator Susan Collins" CNN *State of the Union* 8/26/2018 Egberto Willies "John McCain to NBC's Chuck Todd: I hate the press. I hate you" dailykos.com 2/19/2017 https://www.dailykos.com/stories/2017/2/19/1635559/-Senator-John-McCain-to-NBC- Chuck-Todd-I-hate-the-press-I-hate-you

Russ Feingold "John McCain Was a Committed Leader. He Was Also Really Fun." *New York Times* 8/26/2018 https://www.nytimes.com/2018/08/26/opinion/john-mccain-death-tribute.html

John Baldoni "No Complaints from John McCain" Forbes.com 8/24/2018 https://www.forbes.com/sites/johnbaldoni/2018/08/24/no-complaints-from-john- mccain/#4856339f6545

Chapter 5: Compassion

51. John Baldoni "John Feal Teaches Us What It Means to Serve Others" Forbes.com 9/12/2017
https://www.forbes.com/sites/johnbaldoni/2017/09/12/john-feal-teaches-us-what-it-means-to-serve-others/

Terry Gross "September 11 First Responder Fights on Behalf of Others Who Rushed to Help" *Fresh Air* NPR 9/11/2017
https://www.npr.org/sections/health-shots/2017/09/11/550094607/sept-11-first-responder-fights-on-behalf-of-others-who-rushed-to-help

Wikipedia: James Zadroga 9/11 Health and Compensation Act
https://en.wikipedia.org/wiki/James_Zadroga_9/11_Health_and_Compensation_Act

Feal Good Foundation http://fealgoodfoundation.com

52. John Baldoni "Fostering a Sense of Belonging Promotes Success" Forbes.com 1/22/2017
https://www.forbes.com/sites/johnbaldoni/2017/01/22/fostering-the-sense-of-belonging-promotes-success/

Wikipedia: Maslow's Hierarchy of Needs
https://en.wikipedia.org/wiki/Maslow%27s_hierarchy_of_needs

53. John Baldoni "Homeboy Humility: Growing Stronger and Better By Listening" Forbes.com 12/21/2017
https://www.forbes.com/sites/johnbaldoni/2017/12/21/homeboy-humility-grow-ing-stronger-and-better-by-listening/

John Baldoni "Lessons from Father Greg Boyle: Eating Your Humble Pie" Smart-Brief.com 8/24/2018
http://www.smartbrief.com/original/2018/08/lessons-father-greg-boyle-eating-your-humble-pie

Chris Lowney *Heroic Leadership: Best Practices from a 450-Year-Old Company That Changed the World* Chicago: Loyola Press 2005

54. Gregory Boyle *Barking to the Choir: The Power of Radical Kinship* New York Simon & Schuster 2017

https://en.wikipedia.org/wiki/The_quality_of_mercy_(Shakespeare_quote)
Merchant of Venice Act IV, Scene 1 Merchant of Venice

55. Bob Woodward "Ford, Nixon Sustained Friendship for Decades" *Washington Post* 12/29/2006
http://www.washingtonpost.com/wp-dyn/content/article/2006/12/28/AR2006122801247.html

56. https://www.history.com/this-day-in-history/ford-explains-his-pardon-of-nixon-to-congress

Donald Rumsfeld "How the Nixon Pardon Tore the Ford Administration Part" Politico.com 5/20/2018 Excerpt from Donald Rumsfeld *When the Center Held: Gerald Ford and the Rescue of the American Presidency* (New York: Free Press/Simon & Schuster) 2018
https://www.politico.com/magazine/story/2018/05/20/richard-nixon-pardon-ger-ald-ford-donald-rumsfeld-excerpt-218402

57. Scott Pelley "When Hospitals Become Targets in Syria's Civil War" *60 Minutes* CBS 8/05/2018 (Re-broadcast of program that aired in Fall 2017)
https://www.cbsnews.com/news/when-hospitals-become-targets-in-syria-civil-war-60-minutes/

Syrian American Medical Society https://www.sams-usa.net

58. Aurelian Breeden and Alan Cowell "'Spider-Man,' a Migrant in Paris, Scales Building to Save Child *New York Times* 5/28/2018; Sylvie Corbet and Elaine Ganley France: Macron rewards migrant hero *Associated Press* 5/2/2018

59. John Baldoni "Barack Obama: In Praise of Everyday Courage" Forbes.com 8/09/2017
https://www.forbes.com/sites/johnbaldoni/2017/08/09/barack-obama-in-praise-of-everyday-courage/

"Barack Obama: Profile in Courage Speech: Read the transcript" Time.com 5/08/2017
http://time.com/4770353/barack-obama-profile-courage-speech-transcript/

60. Text of Lou Gehrig's Address at Yankee Stadium on July 4, 1939
https://www.si.com/mlb/2009/07/04/gehrig-text; Richard Sandomir *The Pride of the Yankees: Lou Gehrig, Gary Cooper and the Making of a Classic* New York: Hachette Books 2017

61. Sanjay Saint M.D. "A VA hospital you may not know: The Final Salute, and how much we doctors care" *The Conversation* 3/30/2018
https://theconversation.com/a-va-hospital-you-may-not-know-the-final-salute-and-how-much-we-doctors-care-94217

62. John Feinstein "After the Tragedy of Losing a Son, David Feherty" *Golf Digest* July 2018

Marisa Guthrie "CBS Sports' David Feherty on His Mental Illness and Pill-Popping: 'He's Got Every Psychosis There Is'" *Hollywood Reporter* n7/16/2014, [Award, Golf Channel inspiration]
https://www.hollywoodreporter.com/news/cbs-sports-david-feherty-his-718538

63. Author interview with Dave Johnson 8/10/2018

Dave Johnson Ph.D. "Being Hope" Parkview Health August 2018 (Used with permission.)
https://www.parkview.com/community/dashboard/being-hope

64. John Baldoni "Gratitude: A Lesson in Two Parts" *Forbes.com* 4/04/2018
https://www.forbes.com/sites/johnbaldoni/2018/04/04/gratitude-a-lesson-in-two-parts/

Chris Lowney *Make Today Matter: 10 Habits for a Better Life* (and World) Chicago: Loyola Press 2018 p. 61 [Gratitude quote]

65. Sam Walker "The Plymouth Colony and the Business Case for Gratitude" *Wall Street Journal* 11/25/2018
https://www.wsj.com/articles/the-plymouth-colony-and-the-business-case-for-gratitude-1543162842

Robert A. Emmons and Michael E. McCullough "Counting Blessings versus Burdens: An Experimental Investigation of Gratitude and Subjective Well-Being in Daily Life" *Journal of Personality and Social Psychology* 2003 Vol. 84, No. 2, 377-389
https://greatergood.berkeley.edu/pdfs/GratitudePDFs/6Emmons-BlessingsBurdens.pdf?mod=article_inline

Cheryl Baker "10 Reasons to Say Thank You at Work" *The Give and Take Blog* 9/05/2018
https://blog-giveandtakeinc-com.cdn.ampproject.org/c/s/blog.giveandtakeinc.com/10-reasons-to-say-thank-you-at-work

66. John Baldoni "Gratitude: A Lesson in Two Parts" *Forbes.com* 4/04/2018
https://www.forbes.com/sites/johnbaldoni/2018/04/04/gratitude-a-lesson-in-two-parts/

Chris Lowney *Make Today Matter: 10 Habits for a Better Life* (and World) Chicago: Loyola Press 2018 p. 67 [Cicero quote]

Chapter 6: Energy

67. Jon Meacham *The Soul of America: The Battle for Our Better Angels* (New York: Random House) 2018

Jonathan Alter *The Defining Moment: FDR's Hundred Days and the Triumph of Hope* New York: (Simon & Schuster 2007) [Quote p. 8]

James Tobin *The Man He Became: How FDR Defied Polio to Win the Presidency* (New York: Simon & Schuster) 2014

"A 'Mighty Endeavor' D-Day" FDR Presidential Library and Museum
https://fdrlibrary.org/d-day

68.Jim Loehr and Tony Schwartz "The Corporate Athlete" *Harvard Business Review* January 2001

Tony Schwartz "Share this with Your CEO" HBR.org 6/18/2012
https://hbr.org/2012/06/share-this-with-your-ceo.html

69. David Greene "After an Illness, Willie Nelson Is On the Road Again with His Family At His Side" *Morning Edition* NPR 7/24/2018
https://www.npr.org/2018/07/24/631508812/after-illness-willie-nelson-is-on-the-road-again-with-family-at-his-side

70. Based upon interview and email exchanges in July and August 2018

71. John Baldoni "Pope Francis: Leaders Don't Put Up with Complaints" Forbes.com 7/15/2017
https://www.forbes.com/sites/johnbaldoni/2017/07/15/pope-francis-leaders-dont-put-up-with-complaints/

Website of Salve Noe http://www.noecom.it/corso-di-comunicazi-one-del-dott-noe-a-milano/

Philip Pullella "Pope tacks sign on his apartment door: 'No Whining'" Reuters 7/14/2017
https://www.reuters.com/article/us-pope-sign-idUSKBN19Z0XW

Junno Arocho Neuves 7/14/2017 -Catholic News Service "Pope Francis Puts a Sign on his Door: 'No Whining'" America 7/14/2017
https://www.americamagazine.org/faith/2017/07/14/pope-francis-puts-sign-his-office-door-no-whining

72. John Baldoni "Sister Corita Kent—10 Rules for Collaboration" SmartBrief. com 10.19.2018 https://www.smartbrief.com/original/2018/10/sister-corita-kent-10-rules-collaboration

"10 Rules for Students and Teachers Popularized by John Cage" Openculture.com 4/16/2014
http://www.openculture.com/2014/04/10-rules-for-students-and-teachers-popularized-by-john-cage.html

73. Peggy Noonan "The Wisdom of Oscar Hammerstein" *Wall Street Journal* 3/29/2018
https://www.wsj.com/articles/the-wisdom-of-oscar-hammerstein-1522364613

https://en.wikipedia.org/wiki/Stephen_Sondheim

Craig Zadan *Sondheim & Co.*, (New York: Harper & Row, 1974 & 1986) p. 4 ISBN 0-06-015649-X [Mentor]

"Stephen Sondheim with Adam Guettel". YouTube. 2010-12-07. Retrieved 2014-07-04. [Inscription]

74. "*Fresh Air* Remembers Garry Marshall Creator of Happy Days and Laverne and Shirley" NPR *Fresh Air* 7/20/2016
https://www.npr.org/2016/07/20/486736179/fresh-air-remembers-garry-marshall-creator-of-happy-days-and-laverne-shirley

Note: The quote from Garry Marshall comes from an interview conducted by Terry Gross on NPR's *Fresh Air* conducted in 1991 and replayed after Marshall's death in July 2016.

John Baldoni "Management Lesson: Turn Pain into Humor" *Forbes.com* 8/24/2016
https://www.forbes.com/sites/johnbaldoni/2016/08/24/management-lesson-turn-ing-pain-into-laughter/

75. Abraham Lincoln's Stories and Humor
http://www.abrahamlincolnsclassroom.org/abraham-lincoln-in-depth/abraham-lin-colns-stories-and-humor/

76. Scott Simon "Norman Eisen on Prague's 'Last Palace'" *Weekend Edition Saturday* NPR 9/01/2018 [The story is also contained in Normal Eisen *The Last Palace* New York: Penguin Random House 2018]
https://www.npr.org/2018/09/01/643922026/norman-eisen-on-pragues-last-palace

77. Charlotte Wood "In these dark times, embracing laughter is an ethical choice" *The Guardian* 8/19/2018 [Edited version of a speech given to the Bendigo Writers Festival.]
https://www.theguardian.com/culture/2018/aug/19/in-these-dark-times-embracing-laughter-is-an-ethical-choice

A Leader's Guide to a Better Us

78. John Baldoni "Make Better Your Mantra for 2018" Forbes.com 1/01/2018
https://www.forbes.com/sites/johnbaldoni/2018/01/01/make-better-your-mantra-for-2018/

W1A BBC Television Series
https://en.wikipedia.org/wiki/W1A_(TV_series)

79. Jane Brody "A Positive Outlook May Be Good for Your Health" *New York Times* 3/27/2017 [Wording of Dr. Moskowitz's skills is verbatim as they appeared in the *Times*. Used with permission of Dr. Moskowitz]
https://www.nytimes.com/2017/03/27/well/live/positive-thinking-may-improve-health-and-extend-life.html

About John Baldoni

JOHN BALDONI is an internationally recognized leadership educator, executive coach and speaks throughout North America and Europe. John is the author of 14 books, including *MOXIE: The Secret to Bold and Gutsy Leadership, Lead with Purpose, Lead Your Boss,* and *The Leader's Pocket Guide.* John's books have been translated into 10 languages.

In 2018 Inc.com named John a Top 100 speaker and Trust Across America honored John with its Lifetime Achievement Award for Trust. In 2019 Global Gurus ranked John No. 9 on its list of Top 30 global leadership expert, a list John been on since 2007. In 2014 Inc. com listed John as a Top 50 leadership expert.

John has authored more than 700 leadership columns for a variety of online publications including *Forbes, Harvard Business Review* and *Bloomberg Businessweek.* John also produces and appears in a video coaching series for SmartBrief, a news channel with over 4 million readers. John's leadership resource website is **www.johnbaldoni.com**